THE DICTIONARY
OF DO'S AND DON'TS
A Guide for Writers and Speakers

THE DICTIONARY OF DO'S AND DON'TS

A Guide for Writers and Speakers

by
Harry G. Nickles

McGraw-Hill Book Company
New York/St. Louis/San Francisco
Düsseldorf/Mexico/Toronto

PE
1460
.N5

Book designed by: Paul Kirouac, A Good Thing, Inc.

1 2 3 4 5 6 7 8 9   M U B P   7 9 8 7 6 5 4

Library of Congress Cataloging in Publication Data

Nickles, Harry G.
    The dictionary of do's and don'ts, *a guide for writers and speakers, by
Harry G. Nickles. 3 New York, McGraw-Hill [c1974]* [xi, 211 p. 21 cm.

    1. English language—Usage.   2. English language— *Dictionaries . 3. English lan-
guage—*Idioms, corrections, errors.   I. Title.
PE1460.N5   423.1   74-9856
ISBN 0-07-046502-9

Epigraph preceding page 1 is from *Usage and Abusage* by Eric
Partridge, copyright 1947 by Eric Partridge. Used by permission of
Hamish Hamilton, Ltd.

    Quotation from Arthur M. Schlesinger, Jr., is taken from *A
Thousand Days,* copyright © 1965 by Arthur M. Schlesinger, Jr.,
published by Houghton Mifflin Company. Used by permission.

For Muriel, *sine qua non*

To degrade language is finally to degrade civilization.
—Eric Partridge

In meetings the men from State would talk in a bureaucratic patois borrowed in large part from the Department of Defense. We would be exhorted to "zero in" on "the purpose of the drill" (or of the "exercise" or "operation"), to "crank in" this and "phase out" that and "gin up" something else, to "pinpoint" a "viable" policy and, behind it, a "fall-back position," to ignore the "flak" from competing government bureaus or from the Communists, to refrain from "nitpicking" and never to be "counterproductive." Once we were "seized of the problem," preferably in as "hard-nosed" a manner as possible, we would review "options," discuss "overall" objectives, seek "breakthroughs," consider "crash programs," staff our "policies"—doing all these things preferably "meaningfully" and "in depth" until we were ready to "finalize" our deliberations, "sign on to" or "sign off on" conclusions (I never could discover the distinction, if any, between these two locutions) and "implement" a decision. This was not just shorthand; part of the conference-table vocabulary involved a studied multiplication of words. Thus one never talked about a "paper" but always a "piece of paper," never said "at this time" but "at this point in time."

Arthur M. Schlesinger, Jr., *A Thousand Days.*

INTRODUCTION

This book is meant to help every user of the English language to achieve a clear, uncluttered style. It carries two complementary appeals, one negative and one positive: do not encumber the natural grace of English with the uninspired expressions that encrust the speech and writing of the lazy and the ignorant; and try to make every sentence a fresh arrangement of words, free of faddish whimsy, mannerisms, inexact or worn-out metaphors, and the overworked locutions known as clichés.

Besides originality, good style requires clarity and economy. With these goals in mind, I urge the reader to avoid common offenses against logic or propriety (for example, *between each*), to recognize the windiness of circumlocution and learn how to deflate it (for example, by simplifying *on a daily basis* to *daily* or *every day*), to banish upstart words with twisted senses that destroy exactness (as in *troop levels* for *troop strength*), and even to question the sanctity of certain idioms (*by and large* is one, a relic from the days of sailing ships) that have become detached from their first meanings and make poor sense today.

Jargon, pedantry, pretentiousness, purism, vulgarity—these, too, are treated as spoilers of the language when they obtrude in the text. Nevertheless, this is not a book of technicalities or scholarly precepts. The reader is not forbidden to use a preposition to end a sentence with, or to ever split an infinitive. My chief purpose is to encourage an inventive choice of words to suit each thought as exactly as possible, and this has led me to assemble hundreds of hackneyed expressions—those stale, too familiar combinations or words that hamper the vitality of English like bad habits.

These clichés do not include, except incidentally, our teeming heritage of proverbs, which are commonplaces of folk wisdom too homely to compete with firsthand wording, nor our store of dull aphorisms and platitudes (such as *Familiarity breeds contempt*), many of which have bored mankind since the time of Aesop, nor the often tiresome parrotings from literature—a vast source of stock phrases, especially from the Bible (e.g., *by the skin of one's teeth,* taken from the *Book of Job*) and Shakespeare (e.g., *to gild the lily,* misquoted from *King John*). Slang has also been excluded, but less firmly—excluded because most of its amusing indiscretions turn obsolete before they can be printed, yet selectively included because, once they have gained some popular acceptance, they resemble all other clichés in triteness, their vivacity and brashness lost through repetition: the joke about needing something *like a hole in the head* ceased to be funny at least two decades ago, and now only a dreary inelegance is left in the phrase.

Despite these exclusions, the reader will find here what I believe to be the greatest number of clichés ever to appear in one volume. Many others still infest the language—indeed, no single compilation can record them all—but enough examples are provided in these entries to support this valid warning: the more of them a writer or a speaker uses, the more his prose will lack originality and interest.

If any of my choices and interpretations should be assailed as arbitrary, I must answer that perhaps they are. Certainly some clichés are more stultified than others, and it is the reader's right to evaluate each instance on his private scale of sensibility. I will also admit that there are authorities on English who have kind words for the cliché, calling it by such endearments as "set phrase" and "literary convenience" and defending it as a short cut to quick understanding. I will admit further that every cliché condemned here can be used, and is used at times, by cultivated persons, especially in casual speech or for some deliberate effect. No language can be purged of stereotyped expressions—the title of this book proves that—but an effort to avoid them should be made by everyone who values literate discourse.

The desire to thank my helpers in this undertaking is

frustrated by their numbers. I am grateful to every dictionary I consulted, and to the works of many specialists on
English usage, for direct and indirect enrichment of the text;
despite my frequent disagreements with them, I respect
them all as learned and kindly mentors. For perceptive
guidance on points large and small, I express deep obliga-
tion to my editors at McGraw-Hill. And for very many
random contributions—often given unintentionally—I owe
thanks to nearly everyone I have spoken to or dealt with, or
read or tuned in, during the years in which this book was
taking form. Now that it is finished, only I am to be held
responsible for what is in it.

H.G.N.

Abject Poverty

Cliché, in need of literary welfare in the form of an adjective less fatigued by overuse, perhaps *desperate* or *wretched*. The word *abject*, like certain others in English (consider the automatic coupling of *prime* with *consideration, example, objective,* etc., and see GLARING OMISSION), tends to generate clichés in clusters, vitiating any noun it accompanies—e.g., *abject apology, failure, servility.*

About, Relational

The idea of "standing in some relation to" or "having something to do with" finds compact expression in *about*, a sturdy descendant of Old English. Its Latin-derived synonyms *concerning, regarding,* and *respecting* perform the same task with slightly longer but still laconically single words. With these on hand, it is surprising how many longer makeshifts have been fabricated needlessly and at the cost of litheness in writing. They impede the flow of sentences without achieving a fresh nuance where they appear. Among the most common and least necessary instances are *as concerns, as regards,* and *as respects.* The Latin *re*, as in *the President's policy re minorities,* is an antiquated usage; the archaic *anent* is a silly affectation; and *vis-à-vis,* the French for "face to face"—as in *her conclusion vis-à-vis men in beards*—seldom avoids sounding like the clumsy importation it is. One variation of the *about* idea, *in connection with,* serves indispensably in certain news reports of crime, to define the status of someone arrested or questioned by the authorities but not charged with an offense; but the phrase turns into nonsense when a suspect, on being convicted, is called guilty *in connection with* (rather than *of*) a crime. The locutions that follow are merely other, and generally dispensable, ways of saying *about* (see also AS TO and AS FAR AS . . . CONCERNED):

in reference to   in relation to
in regard to   in respect of

relating to	with reference to
relative to	with regard to
relevant to	with respect to
touching (usually after *as*)	

Abstract Prolixity

The varieties of circumlocution in English include a set of abstract nouns employed to no purpose except to avoid offending by plain speech. They may sound refined to those who use them, but the effect of their use is one of obsequious wringing of the hands or tugging at the forelock—as clerks are supposed to have done since Dickens created Uriah Heep. There is no other explanation, and surely no excuse, for the verbosity in *developments of an ominous character,* when *of an ominous kind* or *sort* would be more idiomatic and *ominous developments* would be the simplest and most natural choice of words. Many similar roundabout usages need to be straightened with equal firmness and cured of their servility: *in an exhausted condition* (tired or very tired); *to a dangerous degree* (dangerously); *in an excessive manner* (more than necessary); *of an unattractive description* (ugly, probably); *of long duration* (lengthy or protracted); *programs of an alternative nature* (other programs); *a victory of small scope* (unimportant); *workmanship of a higher order* (excellent). The word *scale* used in this way is often innocent because it has won acceptance in *large-scale* and *small-scale* to describe activities beyond its basic mathematical purpose in the making of maps: a large corporation does business, idiomatically, *on a large scale.* But in less suitable senses the circumlocution turns guilty by becoming a four-word synonym, and a fuzzy one, for "extensive" or "limited," as in *treating patients on a large scale* and *assisting the aged on a small scale.* It should be stressed that these nouns are not being nominated for a blacklist: the abstractness of *character,* for example, need not be held against its ordinary connotations of fortitude and other traits and qualities. It is only when such a word is used as a substitute for specific information, as in *Steel changes character when it is tempered,* that it sinks into vagueness. (See also DRONE WORDS AND PHRASES and OMNIBUS WORDS.)

Acronyms

A growing threat to our literary sanity lurks in the proliferation of titles and phrases compressed into initial letters and syllables to form independent words. Such inventions are not new. The Second World War'gave us SPARs, WACs, and WAVES. Later the United Nations devised the cumbersome terms that include UNESCO, UNICEF, and the ambiguous WHO (World Health Organization), and postwar geopolitics produced clusters of others, such as NATO and SEATO. Less generally known are the Navy's CINC-LANT and CINCPAC, for Commander-in-Chief Atlantic and Pacific, and the absurd SOPA, for Senior Officer Present Afloat. No one can quarrel with such shorthand intended for use within one group, nor with the shorthand by which scientists compact the names of such devices as *laser, loran,* and *radar.* And by now we must accept *scuba* (for self-contained underwater breathing apparatus), as recent dictionaries do, despite its labored composition. A few other second-stage words may be termed successful: CARE (Cooperative for American Relief Everywhere) proclaims a laudable concern over human misery; CORE (Congress of Racial Equality) suggests something irreducible; PAL (Police Athletic League) offers a special comradeship to the young; VISTA (Volunteers in Service to America) fosters an inspirational outlook; WASP (White Anglo-Saxon Protestant) delivers a well-earned sting; and even ZIP (Zoning Improvement Plan, the postal code) helps us dream of swifter mail deliveries. But no one can—or should—be expected to make sense of the multiplying new deformities. Some of them begin with a pertinent word and dismember it crudely, letter by letter, to produce an equivalent phrase

from the parts, and others begin with a phrase and assemble
a new-word travesty from snippets of its parts:

AIDJEX (gibberish for Arctic Ice Dynamics Joint Experi-
        ment)
ASAP   (Alcohol Safety Action Program, apparently by
        and for fools)
BUDA   (Bureau of Drug Abuse, a clinic that may imagine
        it is working toward nirvana)
DEXTER (a verbal malocclusion for a dental-school man-
        nequin whose full identification is "dental X-
        ray training and teaching replica")
GRAS   (Generally Regarded as Safe, a classification used
        by the Food and Drug Administration, presumably
        excluding marijuana)
HOAP   (Housing Opportunity Allowance Program, a
        sorry pun that would diminish the worthiest social
        project)
IMP   (Interplanetary Monitoring Platform, equipped for
        mischief in space)
LUV   (Light Utility Vehicle—one more proof of America's
        romance with the internal-combustion engine)
NOW   (National Organization for Women—a worthy
        group identified by an impatient fad word)
PET   (Parent Effectiveness Training, to give Junior equal
        rights with Fido and Tabby)
SALT   (Strategic Arms Limitation Talks, without a grain
        of salt in the proceedings)
SIECCAN (Sex Information and Education Council of
        Canada, an awkward designation for what
        should not be an awkward subject)
SODA   (an emetic prescription for Stop Ocean Dumping
        Association)
SPIRENO (Spiritual Revolution Now, one syllable at a
        time)
TOTS   (Tucson's Oldtimers, an Arizona baseball team
        whose players, all past 60, pit themselves against
        the city's Little League.)

Advertisers' English

Not all advertising is cynical or deceitful or in poor taste. Some of it helps us decide where to spend our money, and some of it entertains us with antic characters and slogans. But its only purpose is to persuade us to buy, and all the theatrical trappings—the jokes, the guy-next-door impersonations, the nearly naked lovely women, and the rest—are salesmen's blandishments intended to relax or dissipate our critical assessment of the goods being urged upon us. The tradition is at least as old as the medicine shows that flourished in this country into the present century, traveling with banjo players and stand-up comedians and ballyhooing panaceas and worthless nostrums from the tailgates of wagons. Even today the buyer's search for his money's worth is exploited by the pricing of merchandise just below some sensible round figure—a man's suit for $89.95, an automobile for $2999—to lure him with the promise of an insignificant saving. This method of transacting business breaks no laws, but the impulse behind it often seeks and finds expression in less-than-honorable ways, notably in the slick use of language. Here are some of its techniques, to serve as admonitions to those who would write unbiased prose:

1. *Corrupted Words.* The habit of appropriating noble words and forcing them to carry cheapened meanings can be illustrated by a few tarnished examples: *miracle* has lost its connotation of the supernatural and serves mundanely as the handmaiden of detergents; *custom,* as in *custom tailor,* once stood for something made exclusively for the use of one person; and *gourmet,* a term used as a salute to the connoisseur of exquisite dining, now routinely designates frozen dinners or pet foods. The words *glamour, magic, unique,* and *wonder* have been bedraggled in the same way.

2. *Short-cut Compounds.* A *kitchen-free* dinner can be eaten in a restaurant or in a hobo camp, but cannot, if we value words, be served at home from packages bought in the supermarket, unless it is eaten cold out of cans and boxes and using

only the fingers; and while it seems reasonably clear that a *kitchen-tested* cake mix was made to prove its worth by a professional cook, it is uncertain whether a *doctor-tested* laxative established its effectiveness in the intestines of doctors or their patients. Similarly, utensils that are *dishwasher-safe* presumably are proof against the ravages of such machines, and crockery labeled *oven-safe* will not be ruined by high heat; but what does one make of toys touted as *danger-safe* when *safe*, the only meaning that could be intended, implies the absence of all danger? And what is one to understand by the newest catchword in automobile lore, the *crashworthy* car? It must be like a *seaworthy* ship, which can survive a stormy voyage, but the analogy falls apart if one thinks first of *noteworthy*, in which the idea of deserving or meriting predominates. (For the meaning of laundry that comes out *kissing-clean*, refer to the nearest *rapeworthy* housewife). Exact wording can obviate such doubts (e.g., *a car that can withstand collision*), but that requires wasting words to make the message *clarity-safe*—or, as Thomas Wolfe wrote in literary horseplay, *fit-printable.*

3. *Aimless Comparisons.* It is hard to believe that any serious entrepreneur will advertise that his organization *does more* for your well-being, or that his brokerage *does more* for your investments or that *you get lots more* at his shop, without identifying his competitors and proving that they *do less* or *give lots less.* Yet the empty puffery of this technique is so attractive that political candidates borrow it freely, promising to *do more*—or *the most* if an opponent has pre-empted *more*—for the country or the local dog pound if elected. Varied slightly, the same theme appears in slogans like the *extra-measure* store, which seems to offer three socks at the cost of a pair, and the *total discount* policy, which should cut prices down to nothing. As for what the grammarians call the absolute comparative, custom sanctions it in phrases like the *upper classes* and *man's lower instincts,* but the usage is not so easy to excuse in the adman's *better stores* and *finer workmanship.* If his copy does not answer the question, "Better (or

finer) than what?" it suffers from lack of thought or from a moral shortcoming.

4. *Solecisms and Absurdities.* Of all the sins committed by copywriters, the least forgivable is the effort to reach ordinary men and women, and their children, by resorting to bad grammar and vulgarisms. The trumpeting about a cigarette that *tastes good like a cigarette should* jarred every literate person in its day (see SIMILES WITH LIKE), and since then eager successors have come along—*cookies that are a whole 'nother mouthful* and *kazoo-players are somebody special.* Sometimes sentences and clauses are presented in disrepair deliberately for effect, as in *to kill rats dead* and *to grow one's marmosets up great,* or single words, as in *crisplier pretzels,* and sometimes logic itself is wracked, as in *the music of which you can't get enough of* and *nothing goes with everything like Mama Mao's Bean Sprouts.* Even money, the root of all advertising, suffers the insolence of bad English when merchandise is offered at *a big savings* or for *very little dollars.* The language of advertising is often an unkempt idiom, the more unseemly because it comes from writers who know better but would rather persuade than inform. The wit who named it *ad-glibbing* spoke perceptively. Another name for it might be *the grift of gab.*

Alibi

Not a synonym for *excuse,* though many writers use it in this derivative sense. In courts of law, where the word belongs, it is applied much more narrowly, in accordance with its Latin meaning of *elsewhere,* as an argument that someone could not have been present at the time and place of the commission of a crime. Gradually this strict usage has been stretched to include the idea of an explanation, plausible but false, of any misconduct, with the added nuance (implicit also in the pristine *alibi*) of shifting the blame to someone else. Whether the change came from the underworld or the bourgeoisie— neither group to be commended for proficiency in Latin—

the new meaning has become established and will probably endure as an unneeded counterpart of *excuse*. Let it. But no writer who knows the origin of *alibi* can be justified, so far, in subjecting the word to what is still an ignorant distortion.

Alive and Kicking

Cliché, colloquial or lower. Whether or not it originated in the Billingsgate fish market, as has been suggested, it does describe live crabs and lobsters better than it describes people. It is irreverent to apply the phrase to God, for whom the counterculture has reserved *alive and well*.

All About All

The title of this entry promises more than it will give, just as *all* does in many of its uses. Some of those are too expressive and valuable to be dismissed as clichés, even when they verge on or are fixed in colloquial speech, but the sense of totality in *all* tempts people to regard it as a handy intensive or as an excuse for unashamed HYPERBOLE. The phrases *above all, all along* (whether said of time or physical extent), and *all at once* are good, clear idioms; the first is seldom cheapened to refer to something less than paramount, and in the other two *all* lends strength to the words that follow it, as it does less formally if a person becomes *all confused* or *all excited* when *all hell breaks loose,* after which he feels *all in.* The word is made to overreach, however, when someone is said to be *all business, all ears,* or *all thumbs*—words that virtually label him *not all there.* But, slang or standard, most fixed phrases using *all* enjoy a popularity that exceeds their literary merit. Although *all in all* we are amused by their homely exaggerations, a writer's style is *all the worse* if he goes *all out* for them. *All the same,* and *all kidding aside,* if he tries never to use them *at all,* the effect on his prose *in all likelihood* or *probability* will not be *all to the good,* nor better *all the way around* for his readers, who, *for all he knows,* are *all but* addicted to such phrases. *All things considered,* however, it must be said *in all conscience* that the writer is, *of all people,* the one authority to decide which style is the best *for all concerned,* and which *all* idioms he will uphold *for all to see* or banish from his vocabulary *once and for all.* His work will then, *to all intents and purposes,* be characteristic of himself—or *him all over.* Here are more uses, eight *in all,* which *all told* compose a list he should avoid *at all costs:*

and all, as in *She bandaged his wounds and all.* This is almost equivalent to "and so forth" (compare ETCETERAS), implying further action related to that of the verb. In its dialectal use, the phrase is often a hazy afterthought, as in *wind and heavy rain and all,* but it can also open vistas not suspected by an innocent speaker, as in *hugging and kissing and all.*

all about, as in *what life is all about,* is badly overworked nowadays in the sense of ultimate purpose or meaning—a deceptive catch phrase no more profound or informative than *what life is like* would be.

all . . . is not and similar constructions with the negating word misplaced, as in *All grammarians are not pedants.* The intent is to say *not all are,* implying that some or perhaps most are, but the apparent meaning is *none are.* This piece of illogical syntax, being old and sanctified by idiom, enjoys determined support from serious authorities on English, who must be respected when they embrace such canonized nonsense. They do not, however, reject as unhallowed the less jangling word order that many others prefer. It is permissible (and clearer), therefore, to say *Not every woman looks lovely in a bikini*—an unassailable construction that should appeal to fair-minded writers, men and women alike.

all over the place (or *the lot* or *the map*) is an exuberant colloquial overstatement meaning *profusely* or *excessively,* as in *apologizing all over the place,* or, more literally, *everywhere,* as in *searching all over the map.* This is the property of unoriginal speakers, to be respected as their own and left in their keeping.

all ready and *already*, and the analogous confusion of *all right* and *alright, all together,* and *altogether, all most* and *almost, all ways* and *always*. Since these pairs bewilder mainly those who have not mastered the parts of speech, examples will serve better than analysis to clarify the distinctions to be made. *By the time the others were all ready to go swimming, he was already in the water. The fracture healed slowly, but it is all right now* (ignore *alright;* it is an illiterate spelling of *all right*). *The protesters stood all together in their demands, which were altogether wrong. The minister's eulogies were all most flattering—indeed almost nauseating. The gambler tried all ways of beating the odds but always lost.*

all the further, as in *This is all the further I can walk,* expressing an *as far as* limitation. The usage is a VILLAGE IDIOM, abusing the comparative form and misusing *further* for *farther,* the variant preferred in writing about physical distance.

is all, as in *she likes to read the funnies, is all,* is a colloquial curtailment of *that is all,* which is a curtailment of *that is all that needs to be said in explanation*—a pearl of ellipsis cast in many barroom conversations.

it all, a smart current way of making *it* seem important without limiting its extent or range. The phrase has an honorable place in the annals of cursing—*damn it all, hang it all,* etc.—in which *all* may encompass a small immediate vexation or the whole of space, depending on the amplitude of the speaker's rage. The newer uses are less honest because, for the sake of novelty, they enlarge and blur concrete details. How does the voter *say it all* on election day, except by inexactness, and how does an after-shave lotion *do it all* except by dubious suggestion?

Alliterations

The practice of associating words that begin with the same sound must have begun as soon as cavemen graduated from

grunting to organized speech. The reasons can be no different from those that apply today: a childish delight in phonetic repetition and a mature desire to condense ideas to an
easily remembered pith. Neither reason alone can explain
the prevalence of alliteration, but taken together they help
us understand its value in sloganeering by politicians, merchants, and others not noted for subtle or sophisticated talk.
Even cosmologists compress their theories about the expanding universe into alliterative nuggets—*big bang* and *steady
state*. Choosing among countless earthbound examples, we
may reflect on the bombast in former Vice President Ag-
new's *nattering nabobs of negativism*, the grimness of the name
Ku Klux Klan, the empty promises of *Fine Food* signs along
highways, and one bit of mnemonic patter helpful to travelers who cross the International Date Line: *Monday in Manila
is Sunday in Seattle*. Triple alliterations—*cool, calm, and collected,
fair, fat, and forty, vim, vigor, and vitality, footloose and fancy-free,
single, solitary soul*—are rare, but many others come ready-
made with two sound-linked words and serve durably in
common discourse, but only there; in writing they stand out
like tattered velvet, debasing style. The list given here is
long but incomplete, yet long enough to prove that English
cherishes this teeming brood (see also RHYMING PAIRS and
TWOFERS):

bag and baggage
bed and board
bigger and better
black and blue
blood and bone
boom or bust
born and bred
bosom buddy
chaos and confusion
creature comforts
death and destruction
dollars to doughnuts
do or die

fact and fancy
fact or fiction
facts and figures
fame and fortune
fast and furious
fear or favor (without)
feast or famine
first and foremost
foibles and follies
fond farewell
friend or foe
fuss and feathers
fuss and fume

grand and glorious
grunt and groan
hale and hearty
health and happiness
hell and high water (come)
helpful hints
helping hand
hide nor hair (neither)
judge and jury (to be)
kill or cure
last but not least
life and limb (to risk)
live and learn
man or mouse
mental marvel
might and main
prized possession
rags to riches
rhyme or reason

rough and ready
rules and regulations
safe and sound
saint and sinner
sink or swim
slow but sure
spick and span
stress and strain
sum and substance
trials and tribulations
tried and true
twists and turns
vices and virtues
warp and woof
whys and wherefores
wild and wooly
wit and wisdom
wrack and ruin

Amount

As a noun designating quantity, *amount* is often found trespassing on expressions to which other words are assigned by idiom. In general, what submits to being weighed, measured, or counted in exact units should not be treated as an *amount*. We do say *a large amount of money,* referring to the aggregate, though *sum* would be equally or more appropriate; but *a large amount of dollar bills* employs an imperfect substitution for *number* or *quantity.* The same fault crops up when time is measured: *varying amounts of time* will sound more idiomatic as *lengths* or *periods.* When commodities are reckoned by bulk or weight, *amount* again must give way to terms preferred by usage: it is not wrong to speak of *a substantial amount of cantaloupes,* but the estimate will sound better as *many* or *a great many* if they are considered a few at a time, or as *many crates* or *carloads* if taken in more comprehensive groupings. Other misuses of *amount* may be ascribed to a defective ear: *a small amount of consideration* (make it *a little*); *of their correspondence (a small part); of the preacher's words (a few).* The devotion to *amount* as a point of style becomes absurd when the word is used for pompous elongation—*a numerous amount of people* instead of *a crowd* or *large number*—or when it occurs as simple deadwood, undetected and unpruned (see DRONE WORDS)—*an improvement in (the amount of) traffic safety; an increase in (the amount of) crime; a reduction in the (amount of) funds available; the maximum (amount of) nutrition.*

And/Or

There is no need to wonder where this eyesore may appear in decent writing; it is a freak of language that should inhabit only government, business, and legal documents, none of which can stand as models of good English. A clumsy device, no more literary than the percent sign (%), *and/or* abbreviates the clumsier *and or or* to give the reader one of three choices, A and B together or A or B separately. In *buying books and/or magazines,* for example, the triple assumption is that someone buys either or both kinds of printed matter; but if he habitually buys both, only *and* is needed, and if he restricts himself to one kind, *or* does not tell which. The meaning of *and/or* may be clearer in *eating and/or drinking,* but the awkwardness of the device remains, forcing the mind to analyze how each conjunction—one expressing accompaniment, the other separation—influences the verb. Friends of good prose need not be told that the same thought can be put into uncomplicated English by writing *eating or drinking or both;* but advocates of *and/or* should be locked in a cage with wild ampersands until they can explain *eating your cake and/or having it too.*

Answer

When a problem or difficulty is described, an *answer* cannot properly resolve it—except in classroom quizzes—because no question has been asked. *The answer to traffic congestion downtown is to limit the number of incoming cars. If you are gaining weight, the answer may be in your diet.* To restrict *answer* within its honest meanings, change it to *solution* in the first example and to *cause* or *explanation* in the second. There is an arresting, well-turned thought in *If drugs are the answer, what is the question?* But the man who said *Satisfied customers are the answer to payments on time* delivered a foolish answer without waiting for a foolish question.

Approximation Terms

For the writer who lacks precise figures, or prefers to avoid them as boring (*The fans at Shea Stadium bought* 9847 *Mets buttons*—but who cares just how many?), the language provides a few honest evasions of exactness and several casual or lumpish elaborations of them. Of measurements or alternatives that seem to make no difference, one can say, *six of one and half a dozen of the other* or *as broad as it is long,* but these are tired clichés that suggest a perplexed or undecided mind. The terms *(just) over* and *(just) under,* used with round figures, stand on firmer stylistic ground (but see MORE AND LESS), as do *at least* and *at most.* The others may be grouped under the simple, direct words that they try to replace:

1. *About,* which allows the round number to exceed or fall short of the true one. Preferable to:
around (or *somewhere around*)
around about
in the neighborhood (or *area, region,* or *vicinity*) of
in the *x* range (with upper and lower limits specified; not, as
    in Wall Street lingo, of a stock selling *in the* 40 *range*)
on the order of
or so
or thereabout
roughly

some (with special execrations pronounced on tautologists
who write *some twenty-odd*)
something like

2. *Almost* or *nearly,* used when the round number exceeds the
true one. Preferable to:
approximately
as high (or *as many* or *as much*) as
the better (or *best*) part of
the bulk of
up to

The preferred terms retain their status even in reverse, when
the round number is zero and the approach to it is negative,
as in *almost no one* and *nearly nothing.* Adverbs carrying the
sense of "no more than" can also describe paucity if they
modify positive words: *barely alive, hardly enough money, scarcely
a dozen.* All these are preferable to casualisms like *next to
nobody* (or *nothing* or *no time*) and *practically* (or *virtually*) *nil.*

Ardent Admirer

Cliché. Since *ardent* means "burning," change it to *warm* or
passionate or any other adjective that yields an intermediate
reading on the thermometer of devotion.

As Far As

This phrase often traps writers and speakers into using
windy clauses with passive verbs. In *the best figure skater as far
as the world is concerned,* the intent is to praise the performer as
the best in the world but the effect is to becloud his excellence
with verbiage; and in *the popularity of ice cream as far as the
Russians are concerned,* briefer wording can be achieved by *with*
or *among the Russians* or simply *in Russia.* A variation replaces
as far as by *where* without gaining in either clarity or econ-

omy: *up-to-date police files where criminals are concerned* (on criminals); *politicians ill informed where drug abuse is concerned* (about drug abuse). In a similar form of circumlocution, the miscreant word is *goes: As far as the morning goes, I am busy every minute* (in the morning); *Be careful as far as speeding goes* (not to speed).

These examples, however wordy, are at least grammatical; indeed the *as far as* device is unobjectionable in certain limiting uses, e.g., *As far as I am concerned, the argument is finished.* (Patrick Henry left us the thriftiest and most effective model: "As for me, give me liberty or give me death!") But this good idiom is easily perverted by habitual misapplication and shabby logic, as in *The results are indicative as far as success is concerned*—a pronouncement to be savored only by Mr. Wool and Miss Fuzz. And the worst part of the problem is that some writers curtail the clause in midcourse, almost as if aware that it consumes too many words: *a lawyer's commitment as far as representing a client; a gymnast's difficulties as far as balance; the best in the shop as far as value* (compare ABOUT, RELATIONAL). Such awareness cannot be assumed, but ignorance of grammar can.

Here, for duly concerned readers, are some exercises to be recast in good English:

America is secure as far as national defense is concerned
Municipal bonds are tax-free as far as Federal Income
    Taxes are concerned
Studying helps as far as pupils' grades are concerned
There are no clouds as far as precipitation is concerned
We trust each other where business is concerned
We had no success as far as money goes
As far as to the devaluation of the dollar goes, there are too
    many skeptics
The label is not precise as far as to the contents
She is lazy when it comes to procrastination as far as writing
    letters goes

As To

An artificial preposition much esteemed (and overworked), especially by politicians and reporters. One quality may be cited to explain the baffling popularity of this odd double word: it sounds more genteel than the humble but serviceable prepositions it threatens to displace—*of, about,* and others. The usage can be justified, feebly, in *packages labeled as to contents,* though *according to* would be more welcome to the ear. But in straightforward English, a man is not *pressed as to his reasons for quitting his job;* he is *pressed to say why he quit.* Yet addicts of *as to* insert it even where no other preposition is needed, as in clauses beginning with *whether, why,* or *how: Doctors expressed some doubt (as to) whether the patient would recover. We all pondered (as to) why she wrote the letter. There was no question (as to) how the trick was done.* The noun *clue,* normally followed by *to,* becomes an unidiomatic blunder in the form *a clue as to.* Many other nouns and verbs suffer a similar debasement in the quest for gentility. Here are a few, followed by some of the prepositions that restore their vigor (see also ABOUT, RELATIONAL):

advice (not *as to* but *about* or *on*)
agree (on, about)
argument (about, over)
certification (of)
conclusion (about, concerning)
consult (about, on)
decision (on, about)
disagree (on, over, about)
discussion (of, about)
doubt, *n.* (about, concerning)
expectation (of)
excuse, *n.* (to, for)
guess, *v.* (at)
indication (of)
inquire (after, into)
insight (into)
interest, *n.* (in)
opinion (of, on, about)
record, *n.* (of)
rumor, *n.* (about, concerning)
test, *n.* (of)

At the End of One's Rope

Cliché, specifying the limit of frustration. To be there is the same as being *at the end of one's tether,* with no resources left for solving a problem or perplexity. Both phrases are not only trite but dangerous to anyone who uses them about himself; by dramatizing his self-pity he tempts others to *give him enough rope,* and that could drive him to *his wits' end*—or beyond.

Back Formations

These are usually bastard verbs conceived and brought into the world by mistake. Not all of them are unwanted babies; some are loved and needed and grow up to hold responsible positions in dictionaries and literary works. The trouble begins when someone looks at a noun or adjective and decides, wrongly, that it must come from a shorter verb form. In that moment he becomes the father of a word that did not exist before. (Its given name is always back formation—hardly a sweet appellation for the newborn, but grammarians use it freely, probably detesting the upstart breed.) The creature lives or dies by its worth in serving or amusing others: *to burgle* (from burglar) remains locked in combat with its legitimate brother *to burglarize; to edit* (from editor) has attained respectability and even reverence; *to enthuse* (from enthusiasm) still elicits scorn and devotion in roughly equal measure; *to diagnose* (from diagnosis) flourishes while its next of kin, *to prognose* (from prognosis), languishes, perhaps because it sounds like a nasal deformity. One back-formed rarity, the noun *flab* (from flabby), has all but vanished, but the analogous *greed* (from greedy) lives on for good or ill. Other adjectives have brought forth viable verbs, such as *to drowse* and *to laze* (from drowsy and lazy), but nouns make up the mother lode of back formations. From such as these have come a few verbs that survive with questionable vigor—e.g., *to butle* (from butler) and *to liaise* (from liaison)—and countless more that died aborning, among them *to ebullit, to frivol, to gregare, to hilare, to obnox, to sarcaz.* Out of the spree of innovation came rowdy, funny designations—of Muslims who *abloosh* before praying, winter storms that *blizz,* jokesters who *comede,* cou-

ples who *compat* (and, yes, *coit*), Japanese maidens who *geish,*
Old Grads who *reune,* and banqueteers who *toastmast.* A final
class of bastardly formations provokes not merriment but
irritation by its solemn pretensions. It follows the puffed-out
model of *to orientate* as used in place of *to orient* by those who
prefer clumsy elongations to normal words. One such verb,
to obliviate, in disuse since the middle 1800s, when it meant
"to forget," has been reborn recently as if begotten by *obliterate* out of *oblivion.* In the overstuffed and overworked verbs
that follow, however, most of the leaner, preferable forms
are easy to discern:

administrate	devaluate
cohabitate	interpretate
coronate (crown)	overvaluate
deforestate	quotate
delimitate	spectate (be a spectator)
denudate	

Barnyard Metaphors

No matter how far life takes us from the farmhouse we grew
up in, and no matter if we have never stepped inside one, we
carry its spirit in the figurative and often earthy language of
the barnyard, whose clichés retain at least a whiff, and
sometimes a miasma, of long-accumulated smells. Barnyard
wisdom tells us not to *count our chickens before they are hatched,*
that our misdeeds will *come home to roost,* and that it is rash to
feel *cocksure* about anything, even about how firmly we *rule
the roost.* We classify each other under the labels *good egg* and
bad egg, and speak anthropomorphically of the ineffectual
lame duck and the strutting *cock of the walk,* and of the *hen party*
where *biddies* gather to *cackle* over gossip. Honest businessmen
who *talk turkey* in their dealings end their working days with
a *nest egg* or else—if the finger of fate has *goosed* them—with
a *goose egg* in the bank, or at best *chicken feed.* Of four-footed
creatures, the equine contingent lets us guide our days by

horse sense or waste them in *horseplay,* until we come at last to a *mare's-nest* of disillusion, which is a *horse of a different color;* just as the pigsty projects a life of *eating high on the hog* if we *go the whole hog* or *hog wild* in the quest for profit, then abandons us *hog-tied* financially and knowing that the promise was *hogwash.* Out in the pasture, away from the *rat race,* we can *shoot the bull* at leisure or *take the bull by the horns* and speak our opinions courageously (hoping that they are not the Greek *horns of a dilemma,* one of which would surely impale us). We can also conduct ourselves in the manner of an *old goat,* lecherously, perhaps arranging our escapades so that some- one else will be the *scapegoat,* not caring whether the unfair- ness *gets his goat.* If our victim *smells a rat,* however, or some- one else *rats* on us, we have lost the *cat-and-mouse* game and, unable to *land on our feet,* run the risk of hearing *catcalls* from rude boys and *catty remarks* from human felines. We would be wiser to slink off *with our tail between our legs*—a cowardly dénouement that grows out of the behavior of man's best friend, the undeserving victim of many unsavory metaphors. Any unappealing person, male or female, is a *dog* (*bitch* being reserved, like *cow* and *sow,* for the extremely displeasing woman). The contempt deepens in *a dirty dog,* who follows the rule of *dog eat dog* and in general leads *a dog's life,* wearing a *hangdog* look and surviving on a horrid meal called *a dog's breakfast* or on worse fare *not fit for a dog.* But ever loyal, he *dogs the footsteps* of his master even if he is *dog-tired* and the man's fortunes are *going to the dogs.* The canine status is partly redeemed by the phrase *lucky dog* and by the maxims *His bark is worse than his bite* and *Every dog has his day,* but by these we merely *throw the dog a bone* with a devotion as shal- low as *puppy love.* Although we *put on the dog* for a social splash, and the next day do shaky penitence by downing *a hair of the dog that bit us,* we know that wise men *let sleeping dogs lie* and never try to *teach an old dog new tricks.* Against these massed pejoratives and solemn admonitions, it seems useless to recall a more cheerful cliché, that the barnyard is a pro- ductive *beehive of activity;* the reader is advised to leave the farmhouse and *make a beeline* for the open meadows of fresh words.

Basically & Co.

Sentences that set out to compress or simplify their subject for the reader often sound insincere, or at least patronizing. They use the *in a nutshell* device to imply that there is much more to be told but that it may be boring or (herein lies the insult) hard for one's audience to understand. In *Basically, three companies dominate the industry, Essentially, there are two ways to catch crabs,* and *Substantially, a cat acknowledges no master,* the first word in each sentence, besides being superfluous, impairs the vigor of what is said by alluding to what is not. The reason for such expressions may be the writer's fear that he does not know his subject well enough and may be overlooking some important points or generalities concerning it. These locutions should be avoided because they tend to point the mind in the wrong direction (see also HONESTLY & CO. and TAKE-BACK TERMS):

at bottom
at heart
broadly speaking
fundamentally
in practice
in principle

intrinsically
primarily
principally
to put it in the simplest
  terms

Basis

The name of one method of accounting, "on a cash basis," is good enough jargon for bookkeepers, but it makes a sorry model for other adverbial expressions that have nothing to do with columns of figures—or with anything that helps good writing. As proof we can point to *on a large-scale basis,* in which the last word is superfluous, and *on a daily basis,* which is a tedious way of saying *daily* or *every day*. The *basis* phrase almost always bespeaks a verbal detour that no one should take willingly: merchandise sold *on an ability-to-pay basis* can be made less confusing *to those who can pay;* hotel accommodations offered *on an availability basis* are more attractive *when available;* television coverage *on a live basis* can be tuned more finely to *live coverage;* treatments *on an outpatient basis* should cure the sick more effectively if they remain uncluttered *outpatients*. Other examples of the long and hackneyed way around:

negotiate on an around the clock basis (day and night)
satisfy the world's hunger on a continuing basis (constantly or without periodic famine)
work on a commission or fee basis (for a commission)
strike the schools on a citywide basis (throughout the city)
solicit on a door-to-door basis (from door to door)
buy on an installment basis (on the installment plan)
predict on a long-run basis (for the long run)
speak on a person-to-person basis (person to person)
deploy missiles on a precautionary basis (as a precaution)
schedule on a regular basis (regularly or at regular times)
seek votes on a street-by-street basis (street by street)
help on a voluntary basis (voluntarily or as a volunteer)
forecast showers on a widely scattered basis (widely scattered)

"Bathroom" Euphemisms

No one can estimate, except from private experience, how often people *go to the bathroom* but do not bathe. The phrase is a genteel reference to the elimination of body wastes, a necessity considered too loathsome to speak of directly. Liquid exuded by the skin is affected by the same taboo, but less powerfully: a horse may be said to *sweat,* but human beings more properly *perspire* (in the mad semantics of television commercials, they *get wet*). It will not be recommended here that English should return to the frank four-letter words for urine and excrement, even though recent novels and motion pictures take bold delight in using them, but a protest is in order against the many coy expressions devised for the areas where evacuation takes place. Since we must do with euphemisms, let us accept the simplest and most common: the *bathroom* or *toilet* in the United States (where, however, the whims of usage compel a functional distinction between *toilet paper* and *toilet water*), and the *lavatory* or *water closet* in Britain (the latter abbreviated to *W.C.* and adopted widely in lands where little other English is understood). With another bow to custom, the Army must be allowed its *latrine,* the Navy its *head,* and the yokelry its *privies* or *outhouses* while any remain on the landscape. For vulgarians there is the *can,* recently renamed the *fireplug,* and the *john,* which has been climbing toward full respectability. Many women still have recourse to *adjust my bobbypins, powder my nose, pay a visit* or *use the facilities.* Adults of both sexes may as well be sucking their thumbs when they mention the *little boys'* or *little girls' room.* Toilets in public places bear less infantile but equally hypocritical labels: the *rest rooms* where no one tarries and the *comfort stations* where no one takes his ease. Signs that read *Ladies* and *Gentlemen* are more pretentious than those that read *Men* and *Women,* but both designations are more honest than *Mr.* and *Ms.* or the affected *His* and *Hers.* The utmost in urinary archness was achieved without words by an establishment that displayed two dogs over the doors to its toilets, a setter and a pointer.

Between Each

An illiteracy when construed with a singular noun, as in *between each gasp, layer, page, rafter,* and so on. Two items are required before anything can exist between them, and the wording should acknowledge this need: *between gasps; under* (or *over*) *each layer; after each page; between every pair of rafters.*

Beyond the (or a) Shadow of a Doubt

Cliché, redeemable by exorcising the *shadow: beyond all, any,* or *any vestige of doubt.*

Billiard Terms

In keeping with the lowly reputation of the poolroom, much of the game's vocabulary began as slang and little of it has completed the laborious ascent to standard English. Among the less refined terms is the noun *break,* meaning an instance of luck—a sense that seems to arise naturally from the scattering of the balls when the first player propels the cue ball into their triangular formation. The distribution that results is then a *good* or a *bad break,* though *break* alone serves as a ONE-WAY WORD signifying a favorable outcome, as when a speedster asks the traffic officer to *give him a break* that he does not deserve. (*Dirty pool* from *behind the eight ball?*). Whether some uses of *angle* derive from billiards—*to play the angles, to angle a news story*—seems doubtful, but *to call one's shots* is good pool talk and almost acceptable English. In the United States the word *English,* sometimes spelled *english,* denotes a spin imparted to the cue ball to achieve a calculated rebound when it strikes the cushion or another ball. The term and the technique have been adopted by bowlers and, unrealistically, by golfers and players of pinball machines, who twist themselves into the grotesque postures known as *body English,* "guiding" the ball wishfully after it is too late to control its course. One curiosity about *english* is that the English call it *side,* and that *to put on side* is British slang for airy or superior behavior, like that of a cue ball obeying a fancy spin.

Blessed Event

Sentimental colloquialism for the birth of a child. Now an aged cliché.

Borrow Trouble

Cliché. A colloquial verb phrase describing what worriers do unnecessarily, especially those who fear that they may be *living on borrowed time.*

Bundle of Nerves

Cliché. Transformed by easy extension into another that sounds more Freudian, *bundle of neuroses.* Two other well-known bundles: *of joy* and *of love.*

Calculated Risk

Cliché, pretending to have determined the chance of success after first measuring the probability of failure. Such a feat lies beyond the power of this phrase; the only certainty in *risk* is its uncertainty, which can range in degree from trivial to suicidal and still elude formulation by a slide rule or computer. Used of military operations, the expression dresses the idea of danger in a shimmer of pseudostatistical assurance. (Compare EDUCATED GUESS).

Callow Youth

The adjective denotes a young bird still without its plumage, hence immature. Cliché, for the birds.

Cautious Optimism

Cliché, akin to *guarded optimism.* Fresher adjectives: *moderate, restrained, wary.* Unchanged, the phrase befits one who looks for those equally dim clichés, *a ray of hope* or *light at the end of the tunnel.*

Chapter and Verse

Cliché, used since the seventeenth century in its literal sense of an exact citation from the Bible. Now common also as a FOSSIL PHRASE connoting any documentation or merely supporting details.

Cherished Belief

Cliché. The adjective has become an accretion, rarely needed, as have *firm, implicit, fixed, deep-rooted, steadfast,* and others that routinely precede the noun. If the context demands a qualifier, search out the most specific and appropriate in meaning; e.g., *ancestral, conscientious, pious.*

Couldn't Care Less

Cliché, usually preceded by *I,* occasionally by another personal pronoun. As a rejoinder equivalent to *I don't give a damn,* it reflects an abiding need in American speech for sharp, slangy expressions with which to reject an idea or situation. In the current one only the negative form has meaning, but nowadays many transform it into an affirmative statement—*I could care less*—thereby stripping it (and, momentarily, themselves) of sanity. Its spirit of defiance, however, remains intact, and this makes it kin to two analogous brash quips of half a century ago. One was *I should worry,* which was in widespread use around 1920, and the other was *ish kabibble,* the favorite gibberish of sheiks and flappers of the same period. Both contain an implicit negation: "I am not at all concerned." The second has died of natural causes, and the first survives in moribund condition.

Coup de Grâce

It seems advisable to speak out in behalf of *coup de grâce,* both its meaning and its sound, while there is still time. A French phrase, it means primarily the final, merciful blow by which a condemned man, or a fatally wounded adversary, is spared the agony of dying slowly. Nowadays, however, the element of mercy is forgotten and finality alone prevails. Thus one reads of legislation that *gave the coup de grâce to the housing project,* or of an avalanche that *swept over the Alpine village like a coup de grâce.* The sense of killing, of annihilation, survives without the nobility and compassion that the phrase evoked when knighthood was in blood-stained flower. And as the meaning has lost much, so has the pronunciation; from the mouths of many users now the last word comes out as *grah,* as if influenced by Mardi Gras, the "Fat Tuesday" of merriment preceding Lent—an appalling miscegenation of sounds and senses.

Crackerbarrel Terms

The country general store may be a vanishing institution, but the language of its best-known customer, the crackerbarrel philosopher, dies more slowly. He and his cronies used to sit by the pot-bellied stove for hours discussing current interests—weather, crops, and livestock, or politics, religion, and morals. The store, like the pub in England and the village tavern in Greece, was a gathering place, but sarsaparilla reigned in place of tipples and the appetizers came from an open barrel of soda crackers. Many regret the passing of such establishments, and the feeling is worthy in anyone who would preserve this footnote to our homespun past. If he also yearns for the homely wit and precepts of those days, he can exhume them from the nineteenth-century works of Josh Billings and James Russell Lowell. But if he hankers for the actual words of those clever but untutored yokels—for *by cracky* and *by gum,* for *calculate, figure,* and *reckon* used to mean "think" or "believe," and for such bygone grotesqueries as *catawampus, ornery,* and *spizzerinctum*—his taste in English is retarded. A selection of such usages is listed here; some exist in slang as well as in rural idiom, but they are all to be read through once with due nostalgia and then, *like the feller said,* bunched up and stuffed into the nearest pot-bellied stove (see also PROVINCIAL WIT and VILLAGE IDIOMS):

bang-up job
best bib and tucker
bodacious
chomp
confusticate
critter
cussedness
dander
discombobulate
every which way
fat and sassy
fess up
flabbergast
flustrate
fur piece (= considerable distance)
galley-west
galoot
galumph
geezer
gumption
hassle
hayburner
haywire
het up
highfalutin'
hightail *(v.)*
hoot and holler
hornswoggle
hotfoot *(v.)*

jim dandy
kissing cousin
kit and caboodle
knee-high to a grasshopper
leastways
lickety-split
make tracks
makes no never-mind
neck of the woods
passel
pesky
plum loco, tuckered out
ruckus
see where (= see that)
shebang
shenanigans
shindig
side by each
side by side
skedaddle
smack-dab
splendacious
splendiferous
stash away
two shakes of a lamb's tail
varmint
ways (= distance)
what in the Sam Hill
without (= unless)

Critics' Choices

The job of reviewers is to help their audience decide whether certain books, films, musical performances, or exhibits in museums and galleries are worth attention. To do the job they must understand the art form they cover and be able to tell others about it in clear, literate English. A critic who writes of *polyreferential semantics, contextual dynamics,* or *a fully realized outreach* either does not care to be understood or brings a fuddled mind to his work. He fares better with his stock of adjectives, but even those, through frequent use, lose their power to arouse emotion. Words like *brilliant, dazzling, sparkling* no longer coruscate; *incandescent, luminous,* and *radiant* have blown their fuses; *taut, tense,* and *terse* have gone slack; *vibrant, vital,* and *vivid* yield blurred images. When the subject is sex, punning phrases like *penetrating analysis,* usually *in depth,* provoke no snickers. The simple descriptive words of praise for an estimable work of art—*entertaining, gripping, moving*—seem embarrassingly homely to the critic and give way to the hollow elegance of *consummate artistry, richly atmospheric, tartly astringent,* and to the elusive meanings of *compelling, cosmic,* and *evocative.* (Compare SPENT INTENSIFIERS.)

Crying Need

Cliché, in which the first word denotes an outcry rather than tears. In older usage, this sense of something clamoring to be corrected was applied to various evils, such as *grievances* and *sins.* Now it is found chiefly as a modifier of *need* and *shame.* Adjectives like *great* or *enormous* would bypass the ambiguity and the archaic triteness.

Cursory Glance

Cliché, virtually a tautology. The swiftness and superficiality implicit in *cursory* are almost duplicated in *glance,* which should, therefore, stand alone when such nuances are to be conveyed.

Death Euphemisms

For simple, stark nobility, no verb can replace *to die,* yet the effort to circumvent its painful literal meaning is revealed in many words and phrases stubbornly fixed in our language. Even the approach of death is cloaked in softening clichés: a mortal's life *draws to a close* or *hangs by a thread,* his *days are numbered* or he has *one foot in the grave.* The actuality of death inspires a profusion of awed or hypocritical expressions supposed to disguise the evil. The *deceased* or *decedent* (both are long-faced euphemisms from LEGAL LINGO) is not plainly dignified as being *dead;* he has *expired, breathed his last, given up the ghost, passed away* (or *on*), *departed this life, gone to his rest* (or *to glory*), and so on. If his mourners borrow from the Bible, he has been *gathered to his fathers;* if from *The Book of Common Prayer,* he has *returned to dust. DOA,* meaning dead on arrival, is put to genteel misuse by police officials when they refer, for example, to *a female found DOA in her home.* Plainer people are content with less exalted metaphors for the demise of man: an American Indian *bites the dust* and a cowboy *goes west* after attending the *last roundup.* In slang, both are said to be *out of their misery,* having *cashed in their chips* and *gone home feet first*—a terminal condition designated also as *curtains* or *lights out.* Two other raffish equivalents, *to croak* and *to kick the bucket,* are old, the latter dating from the late 1700s. The newest expression sprang up among our forces in Vietnam, where a killed soldier was said to have *bought the farm.*

Debrief

An outrageous verb, among the worst modern coinages of the unliterary mind, yet accepted without protest in recent dictionaries and sanctioned by general use. One service performed by the versatile prefix *de-* is to reverse the meaning of the word it is attached to, as many believe it does in *debrief.* The compounding works smoothly in such verbs as *decipher, deflate, desensitize,* and others expressing action that can go backward as well as forward. After filling a pail with water one could, by normal formation, *defill* it if the more usual verb *to empty* did not exist. Closer to fact, reporters frustrated by "managed" news stories have set out frankly to *demanage* them, and the Pentagonic mind has fashioned the term *demotivators* to describe the feelings and considerations that drive men out of uniform and into civilian life. But the act of *briefing* deposits information within the minds of persons preparing for a mission, whether military or interplanetary, in a process that is irreversible except by recourse to brainwashing (another contemporary coinage, but vivid and competently fashioned). Any plan to *debrief* an astronaut, therefore, is no more rational than a plan to *decircumcize* him. The usual excuse for a bad coinage—that no other word will do its work as well—is offered in defense of *debrief* and must be endured, however reluctantly. But since a new word was needed for this new way of eliciting someone's experience, some plainer term modified for the purpose, such as *outbring* or *indelve,* or even an unheard-of sound like *spilch,* would have been better than the semantic blunder we live with now.

Different

Often a confusing modifier: a book published in *five different translations* may be offered in as many languages or in five versions using the same language; a patient punctured by *several different injections* may or may not have received the same medication with each needle; and a warehouse that stocks *5000 different items* may be counting duplicates instead of a variety in which each item is unlike all the others. (For *different* misused in an absolute sense, see ONE-WAY WORDS.) Sometimes the word is not so much confusing as inexact: *socks available in different colors* (call them various); *spaghetti served with several different sauces* (kinds of sauce). At its worst, *different* is a sheer waste of paper, a DRONE WORD—a fault, incidentally, that it shares with *distinct* (e.g., *three [distinct] layers of soil), individual (ten [individual] powerboat models),* and *separate (many [separate] grades of rice wine).* Anyone who doubts how useless *different* can be, especially after numerals, should practice reading the following examples with and without it:

choice of two different movies on coast-to-coast flights
interrogation of four different suspects
lights glaring from a dozen different directions
many different styles of architecture
sixty different Federal agencies at work on one problem
travel through several different countries

Different from

For many authorities in the United States, the dispute over *different from* versus *different than* has been settled sensibly. The first is always correct when it precedes a noun, a pronoun, or a few words that complete the thought smoothly *(Their wedding service is different from ours; This dress is different from the one I had in mind).* The second is an expeditious short cut, but only that, to avoid verbosity (in *Morality today is different than in older times,* the use of *than* abridges the clumsier *from that which prevailed).* The British also like *different to,* but in American English *different from* remains standard.

Dimension

Since the days when the earth was flat, or seemed to be, mankind measured physical realities by length, breadth, and a third dimension known as height, depth, thickness, and so on. Then, early in this century, Einstein persuaded us that a fourth consideration, time, was needed to establish the reality of anything contained in the universe. *Dimension* is often distorted, however, out of its meaning: horses cannot be the *main dimension* of a jockey's life, no matter how they are measured. The fad phrase *new dimension* is haphazard talk for any innovation or discovery. We read of a *new dimension in films,* which are not yet effective in the homely third dimension, or stereoscopy; of a *new dimension in travel,* which can be found only in science fiction; and even of a *new dimension in ulcer therapy.* The *new dimension* may be apt as the name of an establishment that turns fat people into skinny ones, but it is absurd everywhere else.

Disastrous Course
Cliché, best suited to believers in astrology, because the adjective denotes malevolent forces exerted by heavenly bodies.

Dismal Failure
Cliché, dismal indeed. Relief lies in the treatment of the adjective: omit it, or call the fiasco *partial, total,* or *catastrophic,* according to size.

Down the Drain
Cliché, a plumber's unpoetic figure of speech for the fate of anything, usually valuable, that is wasted. When the loss or improvidence reverses direction, assets *go up in smoke,* and, if the motion is lateral, they *fly out the window.* Flush away the first phrase, incinerate the second, and let the third one take off.

Drone Words and Phrases
Good writing is economical writing in which every word performs its task clearly and efficiently. If idle words intrude

among the workers, the crowding causes thought and style to lose their sharpness. The blunting occurs when useless brief phrases or single words are thrust unnecessarily, or out of sluggish habit, into otherwise sound sentences. As a first example of unproductive wording, consider *either one of the two,* which is a discursive version of *either one* or *either of the two,* or, if the context permits, simply *either.* Another example is *this is something that will be,* etc., in which *this* and *will* are separated by three dawdling words that add nothing to the sense. A third appears in the offer, usually propounded by a magniloquent speaker, to tell *why it is that Cain killed Abel* (omit *it is that* and get on with the reasons). A few more specimens may be noted, with the do-nothing elements in parentheses: *(in an) angry (state of mind); within (the confines of) the White House; something (else) besides a routine job; in (the) eastern (part of) Canada; a patient (in the process of) convalescing; earnings (in the range) between $2.00 and $2.20 per share; a similar (kind of) effort; a year('s worth) of hard work.* In *they kissed (each other)* the first two words suffice for a normal couple. A selection of solitary drone words follows; all have value when they function in their own right, but as insidious hangers-on they are worthless (see also ABSTRACT PROLIXITY and OMNI-BUS NOUNS):

activity—not *shower activity expected,* as weathermen intone, but *showers expected;* and not *sabotage activities committed* but *sabotage committed*

color—moccasins in tan or brown (color)

figure—a loss (figure) of $200,000

high—a record (high) number of first downs

limit—the maximum age (limit) for applicants

located—a house (located) across the street

mark—temperature above (the) 70° (mark); population at (the) 50,000 (mark)

purposes—water for bathing (purposes); precautions for se-curity (purposes)

radius—within a fifty-mile radius *(within fifty miles)*

rate—a dangerously high (rate of) speed; interest at (an) 8 percent (rate)

rating—a superior IQ (rating)
reasons—for health reasons (delete *reasons* and recast to clarify); for personal convenience (reasons)
role—assume the leadership (role)
stage—foreign policy at a crisis stage *(in a crisis)*
structure—his basic personality (structure)
style—her penmanship (style)
system—belief in (the) free enterprise (system)

Dumbstruck Expressions

It is bad enough to be *at a loss for words,* but to waste words in
saying so is worse. Neither the writer nor the reader gains
understanding from phrases like *inexpressible sorrow* or *indescribable carnage,* through which the writer admits that his
lips are sealed—by laziness or inability rather than by some
code of honor regulating his profession. Writing is not a
proper occupation for the *strong, silent man* of Western yarns,
nor for the *man of few words* (though, if he must write, better
few than too many). Sometimes the burden of comprehension is shifted to the reader by transparent mannerisms—*I
need hardly add, it goes without saying, needless to say* (or *relate*), *not
to mention* (or *speak of*)—with which the writer, in his all-
knowing condescension, introduces a statement that is either
obvious or startling. It is an insult to be told what we already
know, and again an insult to be given a new thought as
though we should have known it beforehand. Less arrogance
is conveyed by the phrases *to put it mildly* and *to say the least,*
but even these withhold candor and rely on the uncertainties of implication. Only a fuzzy sincerity comes through
when a boy says to his girl that he loves her *more than words
can tell,* or when anyone responds to kindness with gratitude
too deep to impart; but self-righteousness invests a sentence that
begins *Never let it be said (of me),* and innuendo trails mutely
after the question *Need I say more?* The serious use of *unmen-
tionables* or *unwhisperables* is a simpering throwback to earlier
prudery. These excuses for ignoring or circumventing exact-

ness are *too ridiculous for words* and *better left unsaid.* Here are a
few other phrases to be given the *silent treatment*:

beggar (or *defy, transcend*) description
beyond the power of words
ineffable contempt
render speechless
too numerous to mention
unspeakable behavior
words cannot describe (or *express*)
words fail one

Echo (Someone's) Sentiments

Cliché, sometimes used in jest. Say *agree with.*

Educated Guess

Cliché, a latter-day catch phrase now finding recognition in
dictionaries, which gravely interpret it as a blend of "experience" and "knowledge" in unspecified proportions. Taken
literally, the phrase all but contradicts itself: if *educated* denotes the *guesser* rather than the *guess,* he is still conjecturing
despite his learning, and, except for the small value of novelty in wording, he could gain the same effect with older
clichés—*informed estimate, shrewd guess,* or, when probability
approaches certainty, *safe guess.* But the viability of this
phrase, to hazard a *conservative estimate,* is still *anybody's guess.*
(Compare CALCULATED RISK.)

-ee

This is one of the suffixes that have escaped from the bounds
prescribed by formal and rational usage (see -IZE and
-WISE) and fled into a jungle of semiliteracy, where they

thrive like any other wild growths. The original meaning of
-*ee* survives in law terms like *lessee* and *vendee,* persons to
whom the *lessor* leases and the *vendor* sells some item. According to the same logic, a man who works at a job is an
employee, and he may once have been a *trainee* and may later
become a *transferee.* His destiny may also make him an *accidentee* or an *assassinee.* In all these normal formations, the
designated person (or, as the addicted say, the *designee)* is
thought of as passive: something is done to him, and by a
clearly understood agent. The coiners, however, deciding
that -*ee* can be pasted on the end of almost any noun, have
given us *absentee, conferee, refugee, standee,* and other words that
show condition or activity rather than the passive state.
These malformations exist and have found acceptance.
Thus we become *acknowledgees* even while rejecting such -*ee's*
except for those fine and correct old friends: *goatee, grandee,*
and *settee.*

Epicene Pronouns

These are the sexless pronouns—chiefly *their, them,* and
they—that presume to speak for both sexes. They are plural
in form but neutral in gender, yet not completely impotent
because they manage to mate abnormally with singular
words and to procreate monstrosities of colloquial usage. In
one of their offspring, *Everybody held their breath,* the first word
is not only singular in number but distributive in sense,
taking the people involved one at a time, so that any pronoun that harks back to it must also be singular. (An analogous absurdity occurs in *Each entry must be mailed in separate
envelopes,* where all the individual entries are wrongly understood to make a plural entity.) With *Everybody* as an antecedent, any pronoun referring to it should encompass both
sexes, but English, the richest language on earth, provides
nothing better than the awkward *his or her,* which only lawyers and other formalists endorse. For a long time this difficulty was met by using the singular *his* in place of *their,* and

ignoring *her* on the arrogant assumption that the female was included as a natural possession of the male, but that was before women became liberated. Unluckily for them, there is still no way to give them equal pronominal rights in such constructions, and the best solution is—probably always was—to replace the distributive word with a suitable noun, writing, e.g., *The spectators* (or *the children* or *the villager* or, if El Exigente is the cause of the suspense, *the coffee-growers*) *all held their breath.* Here are further examples of these mismated and mismanaged pronouns, with suggestions for eugenic improvement (compare VAGARIES OF I):

anyone in their right mind *(all persons)*

each conspirator should get what they deserve (if women joined men in the plot, *all the conspirators;* if not, *he deserves*)

every pupil handed in their papers (if the class is coeducational, *all the pupils;* otherwise, *his paper* or *her paper*)

neither of us had finished our breakfast (omit *our*)

nobody took off their hat (*his hat,* most likely, since custom requires men, not women, to bare their heads)

someone who likes their comfort *(people who like)*

to help an individual to see themselves (first peek to determine the individual's sex, and then adjust the wording accordingly)

Equally As

These two words, sternly forbidden to associate by many authorities, may be coupled impeccably when *as* is a preposition meaning "in a certain capacity": *She liked him equally as someone to talk with and as a partner at bridge.* The authorities are correct, however, when *as* is an adverb meaning "to the same degree": *She found him equally as likable* (in any capacity) is an absurd, redundantly equivalent of *She found him equally equally likable.* Omit either *equally* or *as* in such constructions.

Etceteras

The most common of these is *etc.*, a handy abbreviation of the Latin *et cetera*, which means "and (the) other things," "and the rest"—so handy as a catchall that good writers scorn it nowadays as an evasion of precise expression. The use of *etc.* compels the reader to supply unspecified addenda at the end of a sentence but does not always provide a clear context that allows him to do so. The statement *They went to church and prayed, etc.* may suggest acts of piety performed in addition to prayer but it does not rule out the violation of all Ten Commandments in the House of God. It is true that one lawyer can understand another's *etc.*, and technical and commercial documents put it to acceptable use, but it remains objectionable in any writing that aspires to literary grace, even when its implications are not confusing. If a high-school student writes, "My girl and I parked in Lovers' Lane, etc.," he does not need to elaborate, but neither will his English teachers praise his style. If he writes *and etc.*, he should be flunked in English for not knowing this one scrap of Latin. No, let *etc.* stay banished as a writer's tool and let what it stands for be reinstated. And let the same exile be the fate of the related Latin abbreviation *et al.*, which can mean "and other persons" or "in other places" but can never, except in confused minds, overlap or duplicate the meanings of *etc.* Deprived of these two truncated classicisms, the desperate or fuzzy writer can still turn to simple English—*and so forth* or *and so on*, though not to both at once—but he should not obscure his prose with their even lazier and less respectable equivalents:

and all that	or whatever
and others of that kind, sort, type	or what have you
	or what you will
and such (things)	this, that, or the other thing
and stuff	that sort of thing
and stuff like that (there)	you name it
and what not	you take it from there
or what all	

Exclamation Point

This typographical device enjoys disfavor nowadays, when emphasis in writing is expected to reside in one's choice of words rather than in the punctuation used. To write *I hate you!* adds no perceptible drama to the statement; the intensity of feeling lies in the words, and a simple period suffices at the end. This sort of sophistication, however, which takes pride in understatement, cannot rule out the exclamation point in interjections or short, urgent commands, which without it might seem like languid whispers rather than shouts: *My God! Run! Take cover!* A sensible rule for the writer is to avoid the exclamation point whenever he can, relinquishing it to scriveners of immature prose and the authors of shrill advertisements: *Buy! New, improved! One day only!*

Explosion

A vogue word propelled into many misuses. Its popularity seems to have been touched off by the *The Population Explosion,* a book title that used the word to dramatize the destruction threatening mankind if it continues to breed and multiply without restraint. Although it is difficult to imagine the arrival of any one baby as a detonation, a cumulative proliferation of births can be so described with strong effect. But the metaphor is not elastic enough to stretch over the meanings subsequently assigned to it, which tend to be jolly rather than sinister and to signify swift growth or great size with no menace looming ahead. Thus we are asked to accept the *consumer spending explosion* (good for business), the *cultural explosion* (harmless because meaningless), the *computer explosion* (perhaps they now mate and bear young), and other improbable bangs and blasts. A well-known savant is called a *one-man knowledge explosion.* A bookshop proclaims a *poetry explosion.* A critic speaks of the *explosion of TV talk shows.* After this spatter of hit-or-miss meanings, the inevitable *sexual explosion* must be adjudged an anticlimax.

Facts of Life

Cliché, on its surface a neutral summary of the conditions by which human beings in *all walks of life* exist, but by implication pointing to the most disagreeable of those conditions, as if the full phrase should have been *the hard facts of life*. It is a mystery how this pessimism was transferred to the process of enlightening the young about where babies come from.

Famous Last Words

Cliché, addressed either in irony or as a warning to anyone about to undertake a foolhardy enterprise. If the need to dissuade him is urgent, it is better to say, "Don't" and follow the advice with sound reasons. The phrase differs from *the last word*, which often describes the current state of development in science or fashionable clothes, or triumph at the end of a dispute.

Final Analysis

Cliché, a pompous introductory formula preceded by *in the* and sometimes using *last* or *ultimate* as a substitute adjective. Vaguely equivalent to *all things considered* but more far-fetched because it is borrowed from the chemistry laboratory, where analysis follows strict procedures and yields accurate findings. (Compare WHEN ALL IS SAID AND DONE.)

Finishing Touches

Cliché, applied to the final perfecting of any project, trivial or weighty—a girl's makeup, a hostess' table setting, an Act of Congress or a Papal bull. The phrase, giving no specific information, resembles the ETCETERAS in its poverty of meaning. Some form of a plain verb—e.g., *to complete* or *to finish*—would be stronger than this ornate evasion.

Fishery Terms

For a people who are heavy eaters of meat, we have a disproportionate appetite for aquatic life in our folk speech. We call a grouchy person a *crab,* anyone in authority a *kingfish,* a usurer a *loan shark,* children and insignificant adults *small fry,* and anything huge or impressive a *whale,* as in *a whale of a celebration* or *a lie* (though we stop short, sensibly, of saying *a whale of a whale*). The other piscatorial clichés in English are also a mixed catch, already spoiled from overuse and not worth keeping. In strange surroundings, for example, we feel like *a fish out of water,* but in a more familiar setting we can *fish for compliments,* undertake a *fishing expedition* in a sly search for information, or *fish in troubled waters* to benefit ourselves when others are in difficulty. We also *angle for a job,* hoping that the *poor fish* we apply to will *take the bait* we offer, *hook, line, and sinker.* If we tell him a *fish story,* or our qualifications seem *fishy,* he will look at us with a *fish eye* and end the interview, saying that he *has other fish to fry.* Our failure may look like *a pretty kettle of fish* at first, but then we reflect that working for such a stickler would mean *fish or cut bait,* and feel pleased to find ourselves *off the hook.* We buy a *fish wrapper* and look through the want-ads once more, convinced that there are still *plenty of fish in the sea.* (Compare WILDLIFE METAPHORS and HUNTING METAPHORS.)

Floating Adverbs

The most common drifter among these is *hopefully* when its use fails to specify who hopes. To say *When the war, hopefully, comes to an end* or *After the astronauts, hopefully, splash down,* is to hint that someone is hoping—but who? The writer, the combatants or spacemen, the taxpayer—anyone. In the clouded mind of the misuser, the word stands for "we hope" or "it is hoped," a sense that adverbs cannot carry because they exist to express some nuance of "how," not what is or may be desirable. Thus *fortunately* and *unfortunately* qualify for this free-floating use by signifying "in a certain manner," and several others enjoy good standing for similar reasons: *admittedly, generally, happily, luckily, regrettably, supposedly, understandably, undoubtedly.* (One cumbrous old analogue, *grantedly,* has withered from disuse.) The journalist's *allegedly* and *reportedly,* however, do not qualify because, like *hopefully,* they stand for a verbal phrase, "it is alleged" or "reported," with no one doing the alleging or reporting. Other adverbs capable of muddying a sentence unless they pertain to a firm, clear subject include:

fearfully	sorrowfully
prayerfully	thankfully

Food Metaphors

One similarity between men and pigs is that they are omnivorous, and one difference is that only man can speak and write. The advantage serves man poorly, however, when his language deals with eating; perhaps a pig would do no better if it could speak, but man should be able to express himself much more gracefully than he does about the foods that sustain him and gratify his appetite. The taste sensations by which he labels human personality—*peppery, salty, sour, spicy, sweet,* and so on—are natural and inoffensive metaphors. But such overmasticated adjectival phrases as *finger-licking good, lip-smacking, melt-in-the-mouth,* and *mouth-watering* should be abolished. When his meats are cooked too long, tradition brands them as *burned to a crisp,* and when they are removed from the fire at the right moment they are *done to a turn,* as if on a rotating spit, even if he is serving a

New England boiled dinner. Recipes have propagated other dreary metaphors: *bathe* (or *baptize*) *in melted butter, pop into the oven,* and *serve on a bed of rice* (or on other mattress stuffings, such as greens), sometimes *smothered in onions* but always *piping hot,* with *all the fixings* or *trimmings.* Some cookbooks tell how to *whip up* a mousse that cannot be hurried by brandishing a whip, and a few writers on food burden their directions with a miscegenation of *half-baked* images, as when they start with a *blueprint* (recipe) and *negotiate* (follow) its first step by *antagonizing* (beating) two eggs in a bowl. Not all our clichés based on food *leave a bad taste in the mouth,* but many are at best unpalatable. The following selections, forming a *hodge-podge* (or *hotchpotch*) of slang and standard ingredients—proverbial, semiproverbial, or irredeemably hackneyed— should provide the writer with abundant *food for thought:*

1   *Sayings.*
chew someone out
eat like a bird
eat one's heart out
eat someone out of
    house and home
eat out of someone's
    hand
hunger is the best sauce
in apple-pie order
pie in the sky
take potluck
too many cooks spoil the
    broth
what's cooking?
worth one's salt

2   *Staff of Life.*
bread (= food or money)
bread-and-butter letter
bread-winner (one who
    brings home the bacon)

know which side one's
    bread is buttered on
take the bread out of
    someone's mouth

3.   *Human Touches.*
    Anger and Distress:
boil over (= lose one's
    temper)
boiling rage
fed up
in a stew
seethe with resentment
simmer down
stew (over)
stew in one's own juice
what's eating you?
    Humiliation:
eat crow (or *dirt*)
eat one's hat
eat humble pie (originally *umble pie,* made
    from the *umbles* or

internal organs of a
deer and eaten by
servants)
Sexual Appeal:
cheesecake (and, corre-
spondingly, *beefcake*)
cooky (of a young
woman, favorable; of
a man, often pre-
ceded by *tough* to sig-
nify hard-boiled)
dainty (or *toothsome*)
morsel
some dish
tart (a pastry sweet;
once a proper en-
dearment)
Vindictiveness:
cook someone's goose
dish it (e.g., invective)
out
make mincemeat of
someone
pan (e.g., a play)
roast (e.g., someone fa-
mous or notorious)
settle someone's hash

4. *Mixed Vegetables.*
carrot-top (= red-
haired)
cauliflower ear
know one's onions
lettuce (also *kale*; =
money)

small potatoes (= insig-
nificant)
spinach (= beard)
stringbean (= lanky
person)
tomato (= pretty girl)

5. *Potpourri.*
baloney (= nonsense)
beef (= complaint; also
a verb)
beef up (= strengthen)
clambake (= high-spir-
ited gathering)
cook up or concoct
(e.g., a lie)
duck soup
gravy train
in the soup (= in trou-
ble)
jell (e.g., plans)
meat (= gist)
meat and potatoes (=
fundamental, or not
interested in unusual
foods)
meatball, meathead (=
boring, stupid)
not one's cup (or *dish*)
of tea
peanuts (= trivial
amount or people)
rehash

Some people enjoy *a steady diet* of such language; they *eat it up*. Others, more sensitive to decaying and decayed clichés, will leave them permanently *on the back burner*.

"For" Better, "for" Worse

The preposition *for* figures in several sound idiomatic phrases: events happen *for the best,* pranksters harass their victims *for fun,* and children shoot marbles *for keeps;* slangsters enlarge the list with *for jollies, for kicks, for laughs,* and *for the birds;* and gamblers *go for broke.* Many speak of an unusual experience as *one for the book,* echoing the *Arabian Nights* scenes in which the caliph orders some marvelous happening inscribed in the annals of his reign for the amazement of posterity. No book, however—aside from this one and others of like purpose—should record the intrusion of *for* where it does not belong in literate English. The solecisms with *for* grow chiefly out of two normal source phrases—*(to know) for a fact* and *(to obtain) for nothing.* The first yields *for certain* and *for sure,* both standard but of uncomfortable construction, and *for honest, for real,* and *for serious,* of value only to those who cross their hearts. The second gives rise to *for cheap, for free,* and *for gratis,* transformations that satisfy the ignorant and please the educated who affect offhand inelegance. It is such people (both kinds) who propagate another substandard *for,* the one in *I want for you to cut that out.* The rest of us would say to them *We want you to stop that,* and give them *what for* if they did not.

Fossil Phrases

Various elderly expressions cling to life in English, sustained more by their value as petrified clichés than by a clear understanding of what they meant in their youth. They are not archaisms, which owe their existence to a sticky nostalgia for dead phrases, but have survived for centuries on their own, thus proving their enduring usefulness to those who parrot words uncritically. What, for example, does music have to do with sums of money, as in *alimony to the tune of $100 a week?* Nothing, except that *to the tune of* has been used in similar senses, at least colloquially, since the early 1600s. And what clarity is left in the even older *at long last* (origi-

nally *at the long last*), a phrase that to the modern ear sounds
badly constructed, unless we arbitrarily endow it with its
usual connotations of protracted time and impatient waiting? The worst example of this kind, and the most commonly encountered, is *by and large*. Its present meaning is "in
general" or "broadly speaking," but long ago it was sea-
men's jargon for a way of adjusting sails to keep the wind
alternately ahead and abeam. Few know this today, and the
words have become a highly idiomatic—idiotic, rather—
conjunction of monosyllables that should have been dis-
carded soon after Robert Fulton's time. More such diehards
are selected and exhibited below; most have strayed far
from their first meanings, and all, being incurably hackneyed, are nominated for euthanasia.

at loggerheads (quarreling with words or fists; in use since
the late seventeenth century; origin uncertain, perhaps from
the barbell-shaped projectiles fired by men-of-war into the
rigging of enemy ships)

beyond the pale (outside the figurative limit that circum-
scribes respectability, socially "out of bounds"; literally, a
fence in the fourteenth century, then an area of jurisdiction
such as the *English Pale* in Ireland during the Middle Ages)

by the same token (now, loosely, "besides" or "similarly"; in
use since the fifteenth century, when it introduced a statement sharply pertinent to one already made, as in citing a
second conclusion to be drawn from the same premise)

curry favor (a metaphor that stumbled into existence; from
grooming a horse with a currycomb, the thirteenth-century
meaning, the sense of *curry* changed easily to that of stroking
someone with insincere flattery; *favor*, however, is a mistaken
adaptation of the Old French *favel*, the proverbial fawn-
colored or chestnut horse that typified hypocrisy)

forlorn hope (scant hope or a desperate chance; borrowed in
the late sixteenth century from the Dutch *verloren hoop* or lost
detachment—the shock troops or expendable men chosen to

lead an assault—and soon mistranslated into a piteous plaint)

in fine fettle (in excellent condition; in use since about 1750; until the middle of the past century, while *fettle* retained its early neutral meaning, it could be qualified by *poor* as well as *good* or *fine,* but by now it has succumbed to the rigor mortis of a ONE-WAY WORD)

in the nick of time (at the critical moment; an earlier form, *in the very nick,* was current about 1580 and had the same meaning, but *of time* was added not much later as a reinforcement, possibly because *nick* had begun to falter as a term of temporal exactness; most *nicks* nowadays result from shaving)

kith and kin (as used here, *kith* has weakened steadily since the fourteenth century, meaning first homeland, then acquaintances and friends, and finally, as today, merging into the idea of relatives—duplicating its companion word *kin* to form both an ALLITERATION and a REDUNDANCY.)

leave in the lurch (abandon someone who needs help; in use since the late sixteenth century; derived from the condition of a player who is hopelessly behind at the end of various games, now especially in cribbage; too frivolous in origin for the serious problems—e.g., those of war orphans—it often describes today)

the long and (the) short of it (the gist, summary, or conclusion; in use since 1690—and earlier, from about 1500, in the reversed version *short and long*—without a substantial change in sense; included here despite this astonishing record of fixity because the phrase is awkwardly assembled from parts that contribute little to its meaning)

make no bones about (make no effort to conceal or offer no objection to; the idea of expressing annoyance because there were bones in one's food existed as a metaphor in the fifteenth century; the meaning has shifted from making difficulties to speaking without hesitation, but the image remains colloquial and homely)

out of sorts (grouchy or slightly ill; used with meaning unchanged since about 1620; origin unclear, though later in
the same century the phrase described a shopkeeper whose
stock of merchandise was incomplete, and the word *sorts* was
also applied to a printer's supply of characters needed for
the setting of type by hand)

through thick and thin (loyally under all circumstances;
specifically, whether the way leads through tangled growth
or more open country; though used by Chaucer in 1386, it is
now a mere ALLITERATION with virtually no meaning implicit in its elements)

time out of mind (longer ago than anyone remembers; a
fifteenth-century usage, now literary in tone, that clashes
with the equally ancient notion of being *out of one's mind,* or
insane; to avoid confusing the two, avoid both)

to boot (besides, or in addition to the bargain; an extremely
old expression—nine centuries or older—related to the modern word "better" but now obsolete in most senses; it has
nothing to do with footwear, though the words suggest it)

with a vengeance (violently or excessively; in use since the
sixteenth century, occasionally in a good sense but always
with intensive force; now often found in inappropriate or
puzzling contexts, as in *He counted his money with a vengeance*
and *She reads best sellers with a vengeance*)

Fringe Benefits

Cliché except in its basic sense of rewards won from an
employer by his employees in addition to cash pay. To call
an unexpected turn of good luck a *fringe benefit* is to prop up
a long-withered joke.

From . . . To

An advertisement for a Southern resort offers "everything
from sports to plantation tours." What diversions lie be-

tween the two that are named, and are they sports or tours or activities unrelated to either? There is no answer because the words that follow *from* and *to* denote dissimilar pastimes. In another instance, the dust jacket of a comprehensive book on medicine proclaims a report on "everything from cholesterol to vitamin pills," and again the formula falls victim to untidiness by ignoring such subjects as asthma and botulism at one end and whooping cough and X-rays at the other. The mind has no way of filling these blanks unless the terminals established by *from* and *to* delimit a complete logical series, as in *from A to Z* or the slang term for a formal full-course meal, *from soup to nuts*. Among other possibilities, a list of vegetables *from artichokes to zucchini* promises a thorough catalogue of the subject, and a grin *from ear to ear* fits within intelligible (though hackneyed) boundaries; but to speak, for example, of haberdashery *from neckties to suspenders* is to limit the full range of men's furnishings. At its most expansive, the device inserts *anything* or *everything* before *from,* but the writer or speaker who thinks to bolster his words with such INFINITY phrasing should be doubly—no, infinitely—careful to choose examples that form a straight line of thought, with no oversights or deviations to impair it. (Compare GAMUT.)

Gambling Metaphors

Sentimentalists thrill to the whole arch of the rainbow, but gamblers, believing themselves more practical, set out to find its end, where a *jackpot* of gold is said to await them. They journey in the company of specialized clichés, which flourish in the hazardous terrain of chance but serve only poorly, as hardened phrases, in general speech and writing. Here follows an array of common gambling expressions that have become detriments to original prose. For plunger and piker alike, the guide on their quest is *Lady Luck* (alias *dumb luck*), the fickle temptress who controls *the wheel of fortune,* and they follow her devotedly, hoping to come back *ahead of the game* or at least to *break even*. Their objective is *winner take all,* and they pursue it knowing that there is never *a safe bet* on the outcome and seldom *a best bet*. When the Lady's allure is strongest, they play for *high stakes,* sometimes with their fortune or honor *at stake,* willing to *shoot the works* even *against heavy odds* and no matter whether their recklessness sets them *at odds* with friends and creditors. The risk is rarely as simple as *heads or tails,* decided by a *toss-up* or *flip of the coin.* It becomes far more complicated in the game of craps, where the player wins if he shoots *a natural* (seven or eleven) on his first roll of the dice but on subsequent casts, if he is trying to match an even number—say, ten—can succeed *the hard way* only with a doublet of fives. In honest play, the game stipulates *a fair shake* and forbids *loaded dice.* Tradition permits the crapsman to nullify a throw by calling *no dice* in time, but this is a coward's recourse, and if he takes it too often the Lady will vanish and the rainbow fade from the sky, leaving him *at sixes and sevens* with his fellow gamblers and the house. Though *fortune smiles* at times on a persistent gambler, he can also *lose his shirt* when the smile is withheld—but *that is his tough luck.* (See also PLAYING-CARD METAPHORS.)

Gamut

Forced beyond its basic meaning of a complete musical scale, this word has yielded one tireless cliché, *to run the gamut of the emotions,* which means nothing unless it is accompanied by a defining phrase, such as *from love to hate* or *from laughter to sobs.* Used without specific limits, the phrase meanders between nowhere and nowhere. (See FROM . . . TO.)

Gap

A fashionable shortcut, so short that it bypasses logic. Although the vogue for its misuse seems to be waning, the word has not yet dropped out of the vocabulary of faddists and still merits our notice as an aberration, even while we hope that it will fall into one of its ill-conceived gaps and never come out again. A true gap presupposes an opening rimmed by at least two borders, but if the word is used with a noun modifier in the singular, the reader is restricted to a fragmentary grasp of what is meant. The *generation gap* can denote a fissure or a chasm of misunderstanding between two successive generations, or else the lacuna left by one or more vanished or mislaid generations, and only the full wording with "between" can point out the two elements and begin to measure the distance that separates them. The confusion grows even deeper as gapmanship turns almost every lack or shortage into a one-dimensional gap: a President is castigated for a *credibility gap;* a workingman must overcome his *experience gap;* some nations suffer the shame of a *prestige gap;* industry takes steps to correct the *production gap;* schoolteachers deplore the *reading gap;* the poor exhibit symptoms of a *vitamin gap.* And still the gaps proliferate—the *energy gap,* the *memory gap,* the *quality gap,* the *reality gap,* the *trade gap*—until we wonder whether it is correct to mention the *spark-plug gap.* The *megatonnage* and *missile gaps* are far too grave to bear such smudgy labels, but two others ease the gloom through unintended jokes. One is the *white-collar gap,* applied to a bloc of voters who must have lost a button in the wash, and the other is the *sex gap,* an anatomical allusion that should embarrass, but does not, the gap-heads who mention it.

Generic Crutches

In one of its many guises, verbiage takes the form of generic terms used as supports for words that can stand on their own. When a child refers to his *puppy dog,* he is not trying to distinguish between his pet and the young of foxes or seals, which are also called pups; he is using baby talk that can be found in Shakespeare and Mother Goose ("Snips and snails, and puppy dogs' tails"). He is also wasting the word *dog*—a small offense considering his age (see TOY WORDS), but one that assumes greater gravity when the offenders are adults who say *collie dog* and *poodle dog,* as if naming the breed were not identification enough. It is true that clarity is not always served so economically; we use two-word expressions for certain other creatures: *Manx cat* because the adjective describes not only the breed but the entire Isle of Man; *conger eel* because the first word, despite being the proper taxonomic name of the genus, is unfamiliar enough to require the help of an explanatory word; and *leatherback turtle* for similar reasons, and perhaps to rule out the implication of a motorcycle gang. But when the context supplies the classification, it is thriftier not to mention it: if the subject is primitive boats, do not add *canoe* after *dugout* or *outrigger;* if the subject is fortunetelling with the medieval deck of cards, call them *tarots* rather than *tarot cards;* if the subject is a piano of compact design, dignify it briefly and accurately as a *spinet,* not a *spinet piano.* No reliance on context is necessary to shorten *cactus plant* to *cactus* (it belongs in the vegetable kingdom by right of birth) or *geisha girl* to *geisha.* Of trees, those that bear fruit are properly followed by *tree—cherry tree, peach tree,* etc.—to avoid confusing the product with its source, but other kinds deserve the stout independence of unadorned names; elm, maple, oak, etc. Did Eugene O'Neill write *Desire under the Elm Trees,* did Respighi compose *The Pine Trees of Rome,* did Kenneth Grahame write *The Wind in the Willow Trees,* and would anyone today speak of *the cedar trees of Lebanon?*

Gentle Hint

Cliché. Sometimes the intimation is *broad* instead of *gentle.* Indirection is embodied in the meaning of *hint,* and no qualifier need be placed before it.

Glaring Omission

Cliché, hopeless because it is the least defensible of those formed with *glaring,* like *contradiction, error, mistake,* and *over-*

sight. How can something left out, and therefore not present, manage an angry stare?

Glowing Tribute

Cliché, with the corollary effect of causing the recipient to *glow with pride.* The incandescence of this kind of *glowing* has become so dim that it is time to douse it.

Glutton for Punishment

Cliché, originally slang for a boxer who would rather be battered than give up; also current as *a glutton for work* and other unwelcome impositions.

Grave Concern

Cliché, easily freshened by changing *grave* to *deep* or *serious.*

Grim Determination

Cliché, of the kind that sustained Tom Swift and Horatio Alger's never-daunted lads. This *sterling quality* is mocked today by the sophisticated, but the naïve still use the phrase in earnest. Delete *grim* and restore *determination* to its pristine firmness.

Gun Talk

With or without the sanction of the Second Constitutional Amendment, which grants the ambiguous "right of the people to bear arms," the people have preserved their love of lethal weapons in some of the homeliest and tritest figures of speech. In daily life they *draw a bead on* or *gun for* or *shoot for* intangible goals, *aiming* to win *the whole shooting match* of rewards, *lock, stock, and barrel;* but sometimes their effort, like a poorly primed flintlock musket, produces only *a flash in the pan.* In court they *stick to their guns* under *point-blank* questioning, especially when the questions are *loaded,* and retain an attorney as a *hired gun* to *spike the guns* of the opposition. The bravado that goes with gunfire seems to appeal to businessmen, who like to *line up a target* of bigger profits, fix it *in the sights* of an imaginary rifle, then *zero in*—if possible, *right on target.* Should the project *hang fire,* the sales force comes *under fire,* its record of poor productivity providing the *ammunition* for censure by the angry management, which is *loaded for bear* and ready to *shoot down in flames* any excuses it may hear. Once off the *firing line,* however, the staff is often stimulated by such criticism and, always *keeping their powder dry* for swift action, outdo themselves to make the sales plan *go great guns.* (See also MILITARY METAPHORS and TRIGGER.)

H, Initial

The sounding of *h* at the beginning of a word has a complicated history in English. The Cockneys of London ignore it forthrightly in their well-advertised dialect (*'arf* for *half*), but Standard English generally keeps it (*home, history*), occasionally drops the sound but not the spelling (*honest, hour*), and sometimes cannot make up its mind, especially when the indefinite article *a* or *an* precedes it. Thus we say and write *a hero,* but does he perform *a* or *an heroic act?* Was the meeting between Nixon and Mao *a* or *an historic moment?* British usage in the past inclined toward *an* in such examples, particularly when the *h* was normally silent in an unaccented syllable. But now that they, too, are aspirating the initial *h* in many words, they sensibly use *a* before it. American journalists and educators are less perceptive when they take up the vogue of placing *an* against a robust, sounded *h.* This forces them to weaken or blur the *h* (as in *an hypocritical proposal*). It is difficult enough to pronounce the *nh* in *inheritance* and *Manhattan*, though we manage, but it would be unbearable to have to say (or hear or read) *an hamburger, an ham sandwich* and *an hot dog.*

Haphazard Phrasing

Many flaws in writing and speaking result from muddy thinking; the words employed are usually innocent and unobjectionable until they come together in a phrase or sentence, and then they clash because we fail to see that they are incompatible. If we say, for example, *The price of shoes is costly,* we are confusing the *price* (which is high) and the merchandise (which is *costly*). If we extol the Taj Mahal as *beyond parallel,* we would do better to call it *without parallel* or *beyond comparison,* to avoid botching the hoary axiom that parallel lines never meet. This kind of nonthinking leads to the warped grammar of *two girls as attractive as each other* and to self-annulling phrases like *the city's nicest slums* and *freedom-loving dictatorships.* (See also next entry and MRS. MALAPROP'S LEGACY.) A few similar garbles follow (the possibilities are infinite), each analyzed into its oil-and-water components:

a couple of more people (a confusion between *a couple of people* and *two* or *a few more people*)

almost similar careers (a confusion of *similar careers,* which describes them as sharing many characteristics, and *almost identical careers,* which bespeaks a correspondence at nearly every point)

as strange a looking individual as I ever saw (make it *as strange-looking an individual*)

dollars are the currency of exchange (a confusion of *currency* in the sense of money and the function of money as *a medium of exchange*)

get more for your money's worth (a confusion of *get more for your money* and *get your money's worth*) lay to waste (a confusion of *lay waste*, an honorable phrase used since the sixteenth century and meaning to ravage or devastate, and either *go to waste* or *lay to rest*, depending on how this mental pretzel was twisted)

no wonder why he is so popular (a confusion of *do not wonder why* and *it is no wonder that*)

the fastest-moving city (a community of nomads, perhaps, huddled under an ill-fitting superlative)

the foreseeable future (a confusion about the nature of time; no one can be sure of what will happen one instant from now, and the limitation is not likely to ease until prophecy becomes a normal human gift or crystal balls, oracles, and tea leaves learn to speak more clearly)

the longest resident of death row (the tallest, no doubt, who played basketball on the prison team until he grew too old)

to be in store for higher wages (a confusion of what employees actively expect and what lies passively in their future; the wages, not the workers, are *in store*)

to best prefer (a confusion of *to like best*, which denotes an absolute choice, and *to prefer*, which carries the relative sense of to like better)

to gorge on oysters to a fare-thee-well (whether levity is intended or a mild reproach for overindulging, the effect is equally gruesome; the hyphenated phrase means *to the ultimate point*—in this instance, to surfeit and regurgitation or to death from bacterial poisons)

to suffer a broken arm in two places (probably two fractures in the same arm; possibly separate injuries received in separate saloons on the same night)

Haphazard Wording

This form of illiteracy is found mostly among persons who, in reaching for imagined elegance, defeat their purpose by choosing inappropriate substitutes for the simple, exact words they wish to avoid. The problem goes beyond the homonyms and near-homonyms with which English is so devilishly booby-trapped: *affect* and *effect; capital* and *capitol; principal* and *principle; stationary* and *stationery.* Long and useful lists of such pairs have been compiled as guides for the faltering writer—and any good dictionary, if he will only use it, will help him differentiate their spellings and shades of meaning. The trouble is that he is too lazy to look up a word before he uses it, or thinks he understands its nuances although he does not, and goes on to convict himself not only of pretentiousness but ignorance. Words, like hair, and toenails, cannot be denied their normal growth, but reason and good taste suggest that they be trimmed before they turn unruly. Here are a few of the slovenly alternatives that tempt the careless writer:

abusage—an obsolete and needless form of *abuse;* doubly offensive in a redundant phrase like *abusage of funds for the drug-abuse program*

affinity—an improper substitute for talent or aptitude, as in *an affinity for sports;* except in its specialized senses, the word means chiefly a feeling of closeness between people

burgeon—connotes the sprouting of tender buds or shoots, not a proliferation of mature undertakings, as in *the burgeoning of do-it-yourself power tools*

configuration—a fancy near-synonym, but not near enough, for interior design or arrangement as employed in *passengers inconvenienced by the configuration of the aircraft;* configuration encompasses the whole, including the exterior outline

correlation—more useful to statisticians than to writers; unless tabulated figures are involved, *the correlation between cost and quality* is better expressed as a comparison of the two variables, and *the correlation between automobile pollution and public health* can be improved by calling it an assessment of the damage to the second by the first differential—a technical word used in mathematics, mechanics, and other special disciplines to describe varying rates; misused as a synonym for *difference,* as in *the differential between his age and hers*

emulate—means more than *imitate,* adding the sense of rivalry and striving to surpass

formulate—out of place in *formulate a plan* or *formulate a grand jury,* since the verb *form* conveys the meaning better in each instance

fortuitous—often used mistakenly as a more polished equivalent of *fortunate;* a *fortuitous* event occurs by chance and may or may not bring good luck with it

fulsome—means hypocritically effusive and therefore repulsive; to try to apply it in a good sense, as in *fulsome compliments,* is to deliver an insult instead; often misused for fulgent

intensive—not to be used when only *intense* is meant, as in *intense hatred*

laudatory—misused for *laudable* in the sense of praiseworthy, as in *a laudatory decision*

litany—the name of certain important religious rituals, which has gradually come to mean any enumeration or boring discourse; the debasement is sad enough in *a politician's litany against corruption;* it is crude in *the Howard Johnson litany of ice-cream flavors*

margin—in sports, an untenable term when applied to the complete final score; if one team wins by a score of five to four, the *margin* of victory is one

mitigate—often and unforgivably confused with *militate,* whose warlike meaning *militates* against the gentle moderation implied by *mitigate*

motivation—needless elongation of *motive* in such expressions as *no motivation to commit murder* replete—does not mean complete but completely filled, as a dinner with food; hence ridiculous in *an authentic Chinese diner replete with chopsticks*

service—a workman *services* cars and appliances but *serves* his customers; and a church *serves* its congregation but does not *service* them, liturgically or in any other way, except in the irreverent minds of punsters

totality—appeals to some as more aristocratic than *total* because of its greater length, but *the totality of a man's wealth* is the strutter's version of *a man's total wealth*

usage—as a replacement for *use* or *consumption* of electricity and other commodities, it violates good usage

Have the Courage of One's Convictions

Cliché, envisioning bold action to match bold beliefs, or advising the timid not to shrink from doing whatever seems right. Akin to *do your thing, stand up and be counted*, and *put up or shut up*.

Homespun Plurals

In a language that rejects a plural form for the names of various creatures, such as *moose* and *sheep*, and admits uncertainty about others, such as *fish(es)* and *shrimp(s)*, it is not surprising to encounter abstract words habitually and irrationally used as plurals. The effect is one of undue casualness, even in such acceptable expressions as *a gambler's chances of winning, a philanderer's intentions*, and *an actor's good looks*. It is equally informal to *judge by appearances, make allowances*, or *get ideas about misbehaving*, or to express *doubts, fears, hopes*, or *suspicions* unless one is prepared to specify more than one of each kind. In the phrase *with reservations*, whether the reference is to those in the mind or those recorded by the desk clerk in a hotel, logic would be content with the singular but idiom would probably not. (It is altogether correct, however, to *cast aspersions* and to be charged with *bad manners* when we do.) The same tendency has given us the popular term *Revelations* for the last book of the New Testament; the full title is *The Revelation of St. John the Divine*. So with many other words, these usually cast in a negative context: *he had poor expectations* (or *prospects*) *of striking oil*; *he gave no hints* (or *ideas* or *inklings*) *of what would happen*; *his expression betrayed no indications of pain*; *the government has no plans to use nuclear weapons*; *the scientist offered no promises of a cure for cancer*; *there were no reasons for such rude behavior*. And if *no results of the heart transplant have been announced so far*, the 'patient may be showing *no signs of life*. Idiom or no, such unneccessary pluralizing is inflationary, propounding surplus meanings in an unsophisticated way. *By rights*, writers and speakers who can distinguish between one and more than one will find the idiom *no great shakes* and *have no parts of it*.

Honestly & Co.

In serious writing, especially at the beginning of a sentence, certain stock expressions try so hard to persuade the reader that they put him on his guard instead. A common instance of this, *as a matter of fact*, raises an immediate suspicion that it may be followed by a self-serving plea, or by a fact skewed or trimmed beyond recognition, or by some pugnacious declaration in the spirit of *let me set you straight*. On the principle that no one is considered honest or correct merely because he says he is, the writer should construct persuasive sentences that do not need false reinforcement from such formulas as these:

believe me	frankly
candidly	honestly
depend on it	in all candor

in fact, in point of fact
in truth
rest assured

take my word
to tell the truth

Hunting Metaphors

The killing of animals for sport prompts the division of mankind into two classes, pro-Bambi and anti-Bambi. The pro's consider the anti's barbarous, and the anti's, undeterred by this opinion, still find pleasure in obeying the instinct that kept their ancestors from starving. Either side, in asserting that the other is mistaken, may accuse it of *barking up the wrong tree*. As the debate intensifies, however, both sides may sink deeper into the borrowed phraseology of hunting, declaring *open season* on their opponents, whom they consider *fair game*. Without further *beating around the bush*, here are some other hackneyed hunting terms (compare FISHERY TERMS and GUN TALK):

bait (or *fall into* or *spring*) a
    trap
dead (or *queer* or *sitting*) duck
decoy
drop in one's tracks
follow the scent
get wind of

in at the kill
in full cry
on the track of
pot shot
run to earth
track down

Hyperbole

Most users of hyperbole have never heard its name. The term originated in the classical schools of rhetoric, where it was accepted as a figure of speech that employed exaggeration for emphasis, from the Greek for "to throw beyond" or "overshoot." The practice remains acceptable today, as it was then, if the overstatement is both deliberate and original. The narrator who says, *The boy shot out of the room like a cannon ball*, or the seaman who says, *The waves were riding mountain-high*, does not expect his listeners to think of an exact muzzle velocity or a vertical measurement from sea level; they understand his extravagant language and enjoy it—all the more if the images evoked have not been wilted by familiarity. This is the drawback of hyperbole as it exists in the common speech: it may overstate on purpose, but it relies on words and phrases heard too often to deliver a fresh effect. One who is *dead from exhaustion* inspires no alarm and little concern in others. The verbs *to love* and *to hate*, both signifying strong passions, become pallid synonyms for *liking* and *disliking* when someone is said to *love sleeping in motels* or to *hate jellybeans*. In more figurative language, we overstretch reality with decrepit metaphors when we *lean* (or *bend*) *over backward* or *fall all over ourselves* to accommodate, say, a customer who is *rolling in money* and buys merchandise *worth a fortune* from us. We wrap his purchases and say, *Thanks a million*, reflecting that we *can't get over* his free-spending liberality and *can't wait* to see him return. Of other humdrum hyperboles encountered *every time we turn around*, many fall into the following classifications:

Anxiety
ache for
nervous wreck
tied in knots
worried sick
Boredom
bored stiff
bored to distraction (or *to tears*)
Crime
a holdup (= exorbitantly priced)
a steal (= a bargain)
get away with murder
highway robbery

murder (= disagreeable or painful; in sports, to overcome decisively)
scream bloody murder
Death
die a thousand deaths
die laughing
dying for (e.g., *a drink*)
I nearly died
I thought I'd die
kill (with laughter, as an audience; or to finish a bottle)
lady-killer

make a killing (e.g., by
    trading in cotton futures)
my feet are (or *my girdle is*)
    killing me
use (or *work*) to death (e.g.,
    any cliché)
Fear
petrified
scare the daylights (or less
    rarefied substances) out of
scare to death (or *out of one's
    wits*, or *stiff*)
transfix (e.g., *with terror*)
Geography (Simplified)
all points of the compass
appear out of nowhere
everywhere under the sun
far horizons
in the middle of (or *miles
    from*) nowhere
to the four winds
Insanity
carried away
crazy over or wild about
    (e.g., *horses* or *Harry*)
deliriously happy
driven crazy (or *mad, out of
    one's mind*, or *up the wall* or
    wild)
girl (or *stir*) crazy
madly in love

money mad
Life
for the life of me
fight for one's life (e.g., the
    losing team with seconds
    left to play)
life of the party
Self-Mutilation
cry one's eyes (or *heart*) out
cudgel one's brains
fall apart
go (or *be thrilled*) to pieces
lose one's head
run one's legs off
shout (or *snore* or *yell*) one's
    head off
tear one's hair
torn between (alternative
    choices)
work one's fingers to the
    bone
Unconstraint
all kinds (or *sorts*) of
all manner of (e.g., wild-
    fowl)
all the world and his wife
any number of
anything goes
praise to the skies
sky-high
the sky's the limit

Impact

This is a good word turned chameleon; its meaning is no
longer trustworthy because it assumes the meanings of other
words without good reason. It still denotes a violent bump or

blow by one body against another, and its vehemence is not diminished when *impact* becomes a verb, especially in the new and still unseasoned use evolved from the noun—e.g., a device *to impact* (strike) *the moon* or, by an elastic extension due at any moment, *to impact the bottom* of a disobedient child with a hairbrush. But the basic meaning is seriously weakened when the word is substituted for *effect* (the most frequent misuse), as in *added luxury with no visible impact on cost*, or forced to serve in a phrase of stylish but useless jabber, as in *children spoiled by (the impact of) permissiveness.* Here are a few other popgun *impacts*, with suggestions for stronger wording:

a law that has an impact on crime *(reduces)*
a speech that had an impact on the audience *(swayed* or *persuaded)*
clothes that create a favorable impact *(impression)*
grasping the impact of a new theory *(significance)*
insect stings localized in their impact *(causing local distress)*
no impact on the number of drug addicts *(change in)*
the impact of a witness on the jury *(influence)*
the impacts of computer technology *(results)*
the political impact of bombing urban targets *(consequences* or *repercussions)*

-In Compounds

It seems that any verb can be joined to *—in* nowadays, whether or not the resulting compound fills a need of speech or satisfies the exacting mind. And it is no excuse that the making of new nouns by this process of combining verbs and adverbs is an old diversion of word fabricators, and that many of their creations have settled into the language comfortably, showing hardly a trace of their breezy origins. A boxer suffers a *knockout* and plans a *comeback.* A girl gives a fellow the *come-on* and, after a while, the *go-by* or the *runaround.* Even *know-how,* much derided as a crude formation when it came into vogue during the Second World War, finds a measure of acceptance today, and *flyby,* a useful neologism for delicate maneuvers of aircraft and spacecraft, is admitted without challenge by those who resist innovation. Why, then, object to similar compounds formed with-*in*? Because too many of them have been thrust upon us since the first ones appeared as civil-rights catchwords in the 1960s. In the beginning they served as short, sharp descriptions of social protests and demonstrations by and in behalf of segregated black citizens: a *sit-in* sought service at a whites-only eating place; a *kneel-in* or *pray-in* demanded the same equality in the white man's churches, a *read-in* in his libraries, a *swim-in* in his pools. As a verbal weapon, the verb-plus-*in* device served well in the fight to achieve desegregation. But then it became a fad word and, as fads do, turned silly. Television produced the *laugh-in*, horror movies the *scream-in*, euphoria fanciers the *puff-in* and the *smoke-in* (for marijuana or dried banana peels). Of the many more on record, some need no explanation: *bed-in, cook-in, beach-in, dance-in, love-in, sing-in, smile-in, think-in*. Less obvious in meaning are the *crab-in* (not for grumbling but for feasting on hardshell crabs), the *gay-in* (a flocking of homosexuals in New York's Central Park), and the *slim-in* (a salt-water cruise for the overweight). Until the fad extinguishes itself—and it seems to be burning low already—let us hope that -*in* will soon be out.

In No Uncertain Terms

Cliché, signifying a blunt manner of administering reproof, or *a piece of one's mind*. One variation, *in words of one syllable*, connotes a controlled exasperation in explaining details to a slowhead; another, *in so many words*, refers to an explicit sharp statement, as in *I told her in so many words to be home before midnight*. And a person who *does not mince words* may be more tactless than frank. These expressions, besides being trite, imply an unaccommodating spirit and an unpleasant readiness to quarrel.

Infinity Words and Phrases

Marriage counselors advise their clients that words like *always* and *never* are dangerous weapons to use in a domestic quarrel. *You are always inconsiderate of my mother*, the husband says to his wife, and she retorts, *You never think of me first*. The crucial words in this exchange are absolute, allowing no exceptions past or future, and should be used with great care if at all. The sense of infinity is embedded in such words, and the writer should avoid applying them to finite matters. Eternity hovers beyond the grasp of the human mind, yet we make and use expressions that pretend we have solved the riddle: *all the time; everlastingly; first, last, and always; for an eternity* (sometimes, in suspense fiction, rationalized to *what seemed an eternity*); *in perpetuity*. We express *undying thanks* and extend our vows as far as slang will stretch them—*till kingdom come* or *hell freezes over*. But who will assure us that the electric can opener or the rotary automobile engine is *here to stay*? Only the manufacturer, who radiates *no end* of optimism because his enthusiasm *knows no bounds*. We also strain reality every time we use *every* and its compounds loosely: *Everybody says so; Everything will turn out all right; I've looked everywhere*. Even *the man who has everything* receives presents at Christmastime, after which he is overburdened with *everything and then some*. The same irrationality besets *the car that does everything well*, unless it can mow the lawn and bathe your dog. Eternity can also be extended in the opposite direction, into the past, where the mind fixes it at some primordial point of origin, now *lost in the mists of time*. The most common backward vistas are observable *all through the ages, from time immemorial, since the beginning* (or *the dawn*) *of time*, and—less loftily—*from the year one* and *the word go*. (*Since Hector was a pup* has been obsolete at least since Hector grew up to be a dog.) It is the future, however, that lures us to irrational prophecies and promises. Sometimes they come true, more dependably in fiction than in life. In *As You Like It*, Orlando projected his love for Rosalind beyond infinity with the words, "For ever and a day." He won the girl and presumably they *lived happily ever after.*

-Ize

The suffix is always available for use or misuse, and it will continue to serve the language well or miserably, according to the user. The good examples are numerous indeed—e.g., *atomize, lionize, memorize, spoonerize, theorize*—and can be dismissed collectively with a nod of gratitude. It is the miserable ones that require scrutiny, not one by one because they, too, are numerous, but by roughly sketched families. First among the offending groups come the brats *progenitized* (why not?) by commerce: *unitize, containerize,* and verbs that propagate proper names—let *Schultzize* stand for them all. Next come *finalize, militantize, Vietnamize.* Close behind these stand the *-ize* verbs built on stems ending in *-ic—fanaticize, mathematicize, politicize, skepticize*—all of which yield tongue-punishing abstract nouns, such as *fanaticization.* Then there are the *-ize* verbs that are needed by no one, not even by those who cherish them: Why invent *marbleize* when the verb *marble* has had the same meaning for generations? And why put up with the grossness of *utilize* when tiny *use* can handle all but the few hairsplitting senses assigned to its outsized sibling? Finally, there are the mutilated verb roots fitted with a prosthetic *-ize: permanize* and the recent *euthanize.*

Knotty Problem

Cliché, sometimes presented, with no gain in freshness, as *thorny.* Both adjectives have worked hard for centuries as metaphors, and mercy suggests that they be returned to simpler tasks. Let problems be graded as *simple* or *insoluble,* or somewhere in between.

Legal Lingo

There is an ancient resentment against lawyers merely because they practice an esoteric profession. In the Second Part of *King Henry the Sixth*, Shakespeare draws a caricature of Jack Cade's Rebellion, which flared and was crushed in 1450, and makes one proletarian insurgent say, "The first thing we do, let's kill all the lawyers." Much earlier, in *The Gospel According to St. Luke*, Jesus said, "Woe unto you, lawyers! for ye have taken away the key of knowledge." Modern writers are invited to renew this historic condemnation, not of the profession but of the hideous language that it has evolved in *flagrant violation* of plain English. Only lawyers, for example, can compose a fifty-page document and call it a *brief*. They bewilder the layman with high-flown references to *the said, aforesaid,* and *aforementioned,* and to what may be sought *hereinbefore* or *hereinafter*. They cling to archaic pleonastic phrases *(any and all, part and parcel, unless and until, when, as, and if)* and to redundancies *(cease and desist, false pretenses, one and the same, will and testament)* many of which escape from the courtroom to encumber our daily speech. Other common terms perpetuated by legal lingo, if not conceived in its thick-tongued idiom, include *in close proximity* (near), *in lieu of* (instead of), *pending the outcome* (while awaiting the result), *prior to* (before), *subsequent to* (after), *to the end that* (in order that), and *until such time as* (the first word suffices). It would be a pleasure to simply bang down the gavel on this unworthy prose and see it *laughed out of court*; for stronger action, let us *lay down the law* to those who use it and if necessary *read the riot act*. And for such hardened fugitives from literary justice as may be hereinbelow appended and/or annexed (see AND/OR), *there ought to be a law:*

act of God	letter of the law
a law unto oneself	make a Federal case out of
burden of proof	moot point
day in court	null and void
hold no brief for	open and shut case
law of the land	prior knowledge

pursuant to
stated purpose
take under advisement

the case for (or *against*)
time is of the essence
under duress

Level

No noun in modern times has done more to befuddle plain
English than *level*, a STRATIFICATION WORD that has achieved
tentacular growth into wrong senses and bad usages. During
the Second World War, *level* became a favorite word for
distinguishing bureaucrats from other bureaucrats according
to the authority they wielded, but the word still kept its
sense of a horizontal plane, determining who looked down
on or gave orders to whom. (Its earlier and slangier meanings retain their vitality even today: the *levelheaded* fellow
goes on doing his *level best,* always *leveling* with his associates,
and barbershop quartets continue to moon over *My Gal Sal,*
who is both "a wild little devil" and "dead on the level.")
The present proliferation of *level* must have its source in
some blind need to present facts so as to sound more scientific than they are. This folly leads to the standard ranking
of government activities *at the Federal, state,* and *local level* and
on down to *the precinct* and *grass-roots level.* Even people are
fitted into one or another pseudocalibrated stratum—handling problems *on an adult level* (as adults), working *on the
executive level* (as executives), growing up *at the poverty level* (in
poverty), or simply liking each other *on a personal level* (per-
sonally, or better still, obliterate the four-word phrase). Jar-
goneers who believe that *escalate* and *de-escalate* are better
verbs than *increase* and *decrease* feel predisposed to the use of
level in expressing any quantity in general, and amount,
degree or intensity in particular. Instead of *amounts,* they
speak of *oxygen levels in the atmosphere, vitamin levels in a person's
body,* and *the level of seasonings in food;* for *degrees,* they give us *a
man's level of development, the level of pollution in the ocean,* and *the
level of progress anticipated;* and for *intensity,* they ask us to make
sense of *a low level of combat operations, the noise level at a jetport,*

and *a person's emotional level.* This infuriating word is staging raids against many other words that are its betters—*the level of care at a nursing home* (quality), *troop levels* (strength), *water at the freezing level* (point). In its worst manifestation, *level* becomes a DRONE WORD buzzing aimlessly about:

affordable rent levels (*rents*)
at full employment (levels)
below the surface (level) of the ocean
higher (levels of) prosperity
low salary levels (*salaries*)
prices at the wholesale level (*wholesale prices*)
Social Security benefit levels (*benefits*)

the finest (level of) laundromat service
the optimum (level of) population
understanding at the international level (*between nations or governments*)

Lick into Shape

Cliché, apparently specifying an unlikely tool for giving a desirable form to anything amorphous. The expression is considered colloquial, even unrefined; perhaps it suffers by being associated with other vulgarisms, such as *in good* or *bad shape* (for *condition*) and the drill sergeant's order to *shape up* (behave with military smartness). But to those who know its origin it is a FOSSIL PHRASE inspired by the naïveté of ancient naturalists, who believed that female bears gave birth to "shapeless masses of white flesh" and molded them into presentable cubs by licking at them—a transformation that would require much more than *a lick and a promise.*

Lifeless Points of View

A *point of view* or *viewpoint* can be adopted only by man, and possibly by the higher animals, which may, for all we know, rationalize their actions. The same is true of *standpoint*, which like its synonyms implies a field of perception, physical or

mental, narrow or panoramic. It is wrong, however, to as-
cribe such an attainment to lifeless entities. When an ortho-
dontist prescribes treatment *from the standpoint of dental display,*
he forgets that, however teeth may dazzle, they are not
equipped to assess their environment; and a railroad executive indulges in similar anthropomorphism when he analyzes his company's profits *from a freight point of view,* ascribing
consciousness to carloads. In both these examples the
speaker transfers his own outlook to his stock in trade, and
that confusion leads to the worse error of roundabout phrasing (see AS FAR AS). For example, an official of the armed
establishment announces, *From the military viewpoint, the situation has not changed;* forbidden to ramble, he might have said,
The military situation has not changed. So with *the most popular film
from the standpoint of box-office receipts,* a clause too turgid to
improve without rewriting. Of all such places of observation,
the plainest and best seems to be *from where I stand* (or *sit*) or
as I see it; both sound countrified and diffident, but the findings they introduce are reassuringly human.

Literally

There must be few words that can be classified under both
HAPHAZARD WORDING and SPENT INTENSIFIERS, but this one
may soon attain the questionable double honor. In its sense
of *actually, no fooling,* as in *The child was literally born with three
heads,* the adverb tries to emphasize a fact that needs no
emphasis. But in its newer, looser sense of *impossible but true,*
as in *His followers literally cheered their heads off,* it is becoming
an indefensible usage as hard to countenance as all those
self-decapitated corpses.

Live and Let Live

Cliché, of sententious German origin: an exhortation to tol-
erance and forbearance. The homily becomes less boring in

British slang, in which it is addressed to someone scratching himself as if counterattacking fleas.

Lower Mathematics

The use of mathematical language in nonmathematical writing is a form of bragging about one's erudition. It is not hard to understand, but difficult to applaud, such conventional metaphors as *a common denominator* in a group of people, *a process of elimination* (now almost a requisite in detective stories), and *the law of averages* (including its fuzzy congener *on the average*). Even the algebraic *unknown quantity* does not perplex us when it describes a mysterious or taciturn person. The same cannot be said, however, of algebra's words for variable quantities, which, without straining to define them, we can relegate to the bleakest corner of clichédom. The oldest, *a function of,* has been in figurative service for about a century: success is badly defined as *a function of* hard work; it *depends on* or *varies according to* the effort made. A recent attempt to bring *coefficient* into ordinary use—e.g., the hoopla of the 1920s was *the coefficient of a false prosperity*—is a showy effort to improve on *went with* or *resulted from*—but which? Similar terms that have attained some currency are *exponential* (apparently meant to designate a huge number, though it does not), the abstruse *parameter* (mentioned casually in the plural to connote all solutions to a nonmathematical problem, but also used in HAPHAZARD WORDING for *perimeters* or *limits,* as in *beyond the parameters of normal credibility*), and the more common *progressions,* both *arithmetic* and *geometric* (in rife misuse as the equivalents of swifter and swifter rates of increase). The creaky *frame of reference* is ready to collapse from overwork. The same reproach attaches to *within the framework of,* whether the skeleton of a building or a set of physico-mathematical coordinates lurks in the writer's infertile mind: legislation *within the framework of the Constitution* is a threadbare figure for *in accordance with* or *without violating.* One will be inspired to avoid false mathematics in serious English by pondering a sentence such as this: "The sounds of pursuit made the need to hide increase *as the square of* (italics added) their growing proportions."

Lunch

A word of uncertain origin and wanton evolution. It was in use around 1600, but *luncheon* appeared even earlier. Around 1830, while the longer form prevailed, *lunch* was looked down on as an unseemly stubby version. Then *lunch* moved up to a position of propriety and *luncheon* climbed into aristocratic usage, where it sits today. As fashionable mealtimes changed, *breakfast* and *lunch* were merged into the single PORTMANTEAU WORD *brunch,* which has moved from slang to standard English in the last two generations. But the restless evolutionary process remains at work, for *bruncheon* has arrived to look down on *brunch.* When *brupper* is coined perhaps it will suppress the wayward *lunch* at last.

Major, Minor

These two words seem already beyond rescue, but it may be worth protesting one last time that both words are in the comparative form. *Major* has been twisted to imply absolute importance, *minor* to imply unimportance. *Major* comes from the Latin for "greater" or "larger" and *minor* from the Latin for "lesser." Accordingly, their use raises the question, "Greater (or lesser) than what?" and this should be answered in good writing or at least lie implicit in the context: *a major breakthrough in brain surgery* compares the event with earlier advances in the same specialty, but *a very major statement* by a politician offers no comparison beyond "very more important." By now we also hear one event called *more major* than another, and one problem the *most minor* of all, and feel defeated by the solecistic double comparatives. Are *majorer* and *minorest* lurking in the future?

Make Ends Meet

Cliché, a semiproverbial FOSSIL PHRASE adopted from French and used to connote the virtue of not spending more than one earns, especially if the income is small. More meritorious than *to live from hand to mouth*, with no reserve to depend on, and far better than *to keep body and soul together* in hopeless destitution.

Making Headlines

The headline writer's handiwork has often been discussed and dissected, and almost unanimously denounced, since its volcanic birth during the Spanish-American War, when Hearst and Pulitzer tried to outdo each other in luring readers through melodramatic headlines. By now we accept such journalistic excesses, though never with good grace, because they cannot be avoided; but discriminating writers will not imitate them, knowing that they have become an undisciplined dialect, both in syntax and vocabulary, as cynical as Orwell's synthetic Newspeak. To grasp the extent of malfeasance in headlines, begin with the headline writer's habit of bending prepositional phrases to his needs, foisting on his readers an unidiomatic *in* (*Aide Suspended in Bribe*) or *on* (*New Law Stirs Dispute on Racism*) when space is scant, and awkward padding (*Suit for End of Marriage*—i.e., *Divorce*) when there is space to fill. He cherishes short, impassioned words and feels indifferent to any excessive violence they may connote: in the sports pages, the victor *whips* the loser, who is said to *bow* (it is unexciting to simply *lose*); in the financial section the stock-market averages do not *rise* or *fall* but *inch up, spurt,* or *soar* on good days and *dip, slide,* or *plunge* on bad ones; in reports of crime the police—the *cops,* rather, and the plainclothes *sleuths*—seldom arrest and never apprehend an evildoer but *nab, net,* or *nip* him and his unlawful wares. The catalogue of inbred clichés includes to *ink a pact,* by which we are to understand the signing of a formal agreement between two parties, whether it is a lease for a dry-goods store or an international treaty forswearing nuclear warfare. The need for excitement leads, as in ADVERTISERS' ENGLISH, to the prostitution of dynamic words: trivial problems are presented as *crucial*, often requiring *drastic* action; a stunted broccoli crop can launch a culinary *crisis*, the devising of a cure for bunions can become an *epic* or a *saga*, or at least a *breakthrough*, and the death of a third-rate official or gangster can mark the *end of an era* even if the deceased was not *a legend in his time*. Of obscurity in headlines, one wretched example should suffice—*Goat Blood Guards Jet*, which headed a news report about the sacrifice of a goat in an Asian land to invoke divine benevolence on its first *Boeing 727*. Halfway between obscurity and absurdity lie the headlines that tolerate REDUNDANCIES—*Plant Hit by Strike*—and those that backfire with secondary meanings—*Health Care for Aged Mushrooms*. The pun deliberately made infests today's headlines, delighting the writer and his editor—but whom besides? There is more slapstick than news in *Bus Use Skids, Coffee Sales Perk Up*, and *Wintry Weather Snowballs*.

Here follows a selective primer of headline usage, limited to the most arbitrarily abused part of speech, the verb. For the benefit of the bewildered, analogues in Oldspeak head each group.

Approve	rip
bless	score
hail	*Connect or implicate*
laud	link
OK	tie to
Assail or dispute	*Consider or debate*
blast	eye
clash (with)	mull
flay	scan
hit	weigh
lash	*Increase*
rap (now also hip-talk for a	boost
friendly chat)	bulge

hike   pare
lift   slash
up (e.g., taxes)   slice
Reduce   trim
cut

Man in the Street

Cliché, designating the ordinary man as he was imagined more than a century ago, before the statisticians stippled him with decimal points and renamed him the *average man.* Both are mythical creatures, like *John Doe* and *Joe Blow.* In Wall Street his counterpart is the *little guy* with a pittance to invest. In 1942 Vice President Henry A. Wallace exalted him as the *common man* who would benefit from the affluence of the twentieth century, but few were attracted by the slogan, which, however well meant, implies mediocrity and not distinction. Nearly everyone would rather be *a man about town.*

Mangled Greek Words

Certain words from the Greek have behaved like Trojan Horses in our midst, treacherously wrecking what they touch. One is *electron,* the word for *amber,* which gave us *electricity,* from the static charge the fossil resin acquires when rubbed with a cloth, and which later developed into *electronics* and ultimately into an untamed profusion of business names trading on the syllable *-tron,* which has no meaning of its own: *Textron, Ticketron,* and (so far unattested) *Chickentron.* The word *automatic,* also of Greek origin, saw duty in the once popular *automat* cafeterias and still works overtime to bring us the blessings of *automation,* but today just one of its syllables, *-mat-,* seems to confer magical powers on any product christened with it: the *laundromat* is already with us, and a *dialamatic* dictionary *or sleepomatic* pillow may come along soon. A third word, not ancient but coined from authentic Greek elements, is *panorama* for total view; now merchants graft its rear end *-orama* (sometimes altered to *-arama*) indiscriminately on such commodities as *beer-, dress-* and *tool-,* or practice the inept surgery that yields *lobsterama.* A fourth is *marathon,* taken from the plain on which the Greeks routed the Persians in 490 B.C. and from which a lengendary runner ran more than twenty-six miles to Athens with news of the victory. In its latter-day rebirth the word designates a long-distance foot race in the Olympic Games or any protracted test of endurance, such as the idiotic *marathon dance* competitions of the 1920s, but again the butchers have hacked it in two, preserving only the backside—as in *jogathon, telethon,* and possibly, as X-rated movies become better than ever, *sexathon*—and passing the ugly-mongrel words along as if they had issued from the Trojan Horse's mouth.

Manners of Speaking

Competent writers of fiction make up dialogue that reads like natural speech, and news reporters learn from cubhood that they must quote their sources exactly, again reflecting natural speech. Exposed to either form of prose, the reader seldom wonders what was said or implied or left unsaid, nor how the words were delivered. A serious fault develops, however, when the writer feels that it is not enough to have his speaker *say* the quoted words, as if so simple a verb must fail to be effective, and discards it in favor of strange and mostly unnecessary elaborations. A few variations of *say* are proper if needed to describe actual ways of speaking: *cry, exclaim, mumble, mutter, shout, whisper, yell.* In more formal contexts the speaker may *comment, declare, state,* or *observe;* but it is a misuse when he is made to *indicate* a forthright statement, and a cheap dramatization if he is forced to *claim* or *maintain* what he is merely uttering, or to *confide* his words when there is nothing confidential about them. An interrogative statement, directly quoted, is best followed by *ask* or *inquire,* more vigorously by *demand*, and only maladroitly by the mannered noun-verbs *query* and *question*. A second speaker may *answer*, *reply*, or even *retort*, and at any appropriate point he may *cut in* or *interrupt*, after which the first speaker may *continue*, *go on*, or *resume*. All these verbs, and some others like them, report honestly and inconspicuously. Mannered substitutes must be condemned because they go without *saying*. They fall into three classes, recorded below with and without examples of overexplained quotations, so that readers can make up their own:

1. Verbs that expose the speaker's intent but do not describe speech. Models: "You lie," he accused; "You win," she capitulated; "I don't like this," he disapproved.

acknowledge	emphasize
admonish	explain
allow	greet
amplify	grumble
cajole	lament
caution	needle
chide	scoff
commiserate	soothe
complain	stress
concede	sympathize
confess	venture
counter	warn

2. Verbs representing various noises—human or other—that either interfere with clear speech or make articulation impossible. Models: "Come here," he barked; "Mother is dead," he choked; "That beer hit the spot," he exhaled.

bellow	croak
boom	explode
bubble	fume
chirp	giggle
chortle	groan
chuckle	growl

grunt	snap
guffaw	snarl
huff	sniff
laugh	snort
moan	sob
pipe	spit
purr	thunder
scream	wail
screech	whimper
shrill	yawn
sigh	

3. Verbs of action that suggest no sound, least of all speech. Models: "Hello," he grinned; "Coffee?" she held out; "Who cares?" he shrugged. Other silent quotations have been constructed with *frown, grimace, nod, nudge, smile, squirm,* etc.

Matter

Without attacking the sound uses of the noun *matter,* which outnumber the unsound, one can point to many phrases in which it functions either as a tired workhorse or as an uninvited presence. Nearly everyone overworks *as a matter of fact, as a matter of course,* and *for that matter,* along with *a matter of form* or *of life and death,* and tries too often, with pitiful fumbling, to penetrate *to the bottom, core, crux, fact, heart, root,* or *truth of the matter.* The unneeded uses arise out of one of the word's several meanings—an indefinite quantity or duration—as in *a matter of time.* When this convenient and irreproachable idiom becomes an excuse for tumid effigies of itself, the writer should scrutinize them with excision in mind. If an event takes place in seconds or minutes or hours, it is wasteful to say *in a matter of seconds,* etc. Nor is time the only subject abused by this sprawling mannerism. Examine these examples: *Digging ditches is a matter of hard work; The election is a matter of history now; Weather forecasting is a matter of guesswork.* In each of the three the *matter* phrase can be deleted without loss of meaning and with an improvement in concise expression. It is conceded that such a deletion sometimes demands other words to round out the sense—e.g., *Making money in common stocks is a matter of shrewd timing*—but in this instance the substitution of *involves* or *depends on* results in a more forceful sentence, and in most other instances a better verb awaits the speaker or writer who is wary of *a matter of.*

Medical Metaphors

Since it is rare for any of us to be *in perfect health*, perhaps we are the victims of a latent hypochondria that reveals itself in references to illness, remembered or feared, when we write and speak. Politicians speak of such figurative ailments as *anemic campaign contributions, hardening of the political arteries, overdoses of welfare, slowing of the social reflexes,* and *transfusions of money*—all beset by unexpected *side effects.* Among financiers, when the dollar loses ground in the international money markets, it suffers a *sinking spell* heralded by various *economic symptoms,* and the seizure must *run its course* unless there is emergency *pulse-taking* in banking circles (conducted *at fever pitch*) that leads to the *prescription* of some *desperate remedy,* like the *bitter pill* of devaluation. A few common medical expressions may be loosely termed *strong medicine* compared to the good they do: when a dispute or a problem *comes to a head* it should behave like a boil or abscess and begin discharging pus; the *seven-year itch,* now a joke about the boredom of monogamy, is the folk name for scabies or mange, which is caused by mites that burrow into the skin and lay eggs there; and other serious disorders are taken all too lightly when we describe an angry person as *having a convulsion, a fit,* or *a heart attack.* The *sick humor* of a few years ago is dead or healed at last, but the subconscious hypochondria persists in several *measly* locutions: *doctor's orders* (a hackneyed excuse for a strong drink); *just what the doctor ordered* (including non-alcoholic satisfactions); *to be given a dose of one's own medicine* (be repaid in kind, vengefully); *to take one's medicine* (like a man); and *you're the doctor* (a concession to another's wishes or opinion). From ancient times onward the world has been hearing, when a solution to a difficulty is rejected, that *the cure is worse than the disease.* So the language repines on its *bed of pain,* enduring this *rash* of medical clichés.

Meet One's Match

Cliché, not easily reworded, though the effort should be made. It is helpful to remember that, if two antagonists compete at witticisms or insults and neither prevails, the outcome is a draw. The implication that one of the two felt sure of winning, but did not, should also be preserved. A loser, according to an associated cliché, has *met his master.*

Memento

This means chiefly a keepsake or reminder. It comes to us intact from Latin, as an imperative form of the verb meaning "to remember," and thus commands the *mem*ory to action. Those who use the spelling *momento* are forgetting not only their Latin but their English.

Menu Blunders

The efforts to glorify the day's offerings with pseudopoetry— the *dew-fresh salad,* the *savory morsels,* the *whisper of garlic*—are not at issue here; we can be amused by stumbling imagery provided it stops short of turning our stomach. Nor are the careless misprints, some of which sink to the depths of anti-poetry, as in *spewed prunes.* What does matter is the debasement of the good names of foods by the addition of generic terms. Whoever writes *pumpernickel bread* has not been in-

formed that the word *pumpernickel* designates a certain kind
of bread and needs no second-helping explanation. He also
tempts us with a *rice pilaf,* as though *pilaf* were not a rice dish
to begin with (the *wheat pilaf* encountered nowadays acquired its name by culinary plagiarism). We find *cup* appended to *demitasse, nut* to *filbert, pie* to *pizza,* and even *soup* to
clam chowder. Cheese is inserted after *Roquefort* and *whiskey* after
Bourbon, and *port* and *sherry* are diluted with watery post-
script *wine,* defining what requires no definition. Foods bear-
ing unfamiliar foreign names bring out the worst bilingual
tautologies, as in *coq au vin chicken, crêpes Suzette pancakes, filet
mignon steak, roast beef with au jus gravy, soupe du jour of the day,*
and *veal cutlet Wienerschnitzel.* No one knows how many
Americans order *shrimp scampi* in the belief that *scampi* denotes a recipe for pungent shrimp, although it means the
prized Italian prawns (superior to shrimp) that can be
cooked in many ways.

Messy Possessives

The needs of casual language are satisfied if its words are
understood, at least roughly, by a casual scrutiny. The critical mind, which analyzes and is sensitive to implications, is
not so easily lulled. It requires writers and speakers to say
what they mean in words that do not trail untidy shreds of
other senses. In the handling of some possessive phrases, this
principle of clarity may make a brief circumlocution necessary, but it is better to squander a few extra words than to
muddle along in ambiguity. There is an appealing compact-
ness in, for example, *Literature has influenced the quality of all our
lives,* until we ask how many lives fall to the lot of anyone
(surely not nine), and realize that the last part of the sentence should read, more formally but with no risk of ridicule, *the life quality of all of us.* The same deceptiveness resides
in *All the others' faces went white* (well, Janus had two faces),
Some of their heads were bald (Cerberus had three heads), and
We stared with all our eyes (Argus had a hundred). The words

either and *neither* create similar problems: *We can go in either of their cars* (write the car of either one, but, if one or both own two cars, postpone the trip and construct a new sentence); *The judge heeded neither of the defendants' pleas* (the plea or pleas of neither defendant, depending on the number put forth by each, unless there were more than two defendants, each pleading twice). The confusion seems to abate in the remark *both (of) your brothers,* but only if it is addressed to someone who has two brothers; it recedes into chaos when it refers to all the brothers of two persons. *Both* can rudely upset propriety in an expression like *Regards to both your wives,* implying bigamy even when the greeting is distributive and separate husbands are the messengers. Some confused possessives are at least as awkward as they are irrational—e.g., *deeds done before all of your times, one of my best friends' mother*—but all need the tidying hand of revision.

Military Metaphors

"A splendid little war." With these words John Hay, Secretary of State under President McKinley, exulted in the armed conflict of 1898 between Spain and the United States. Today there is neither littleness nor splendor left in warfare that will reckon casualties in *megadeaths* (millions of lives lost) caused by the *destructive yield* (like a hideous crop) of hydrogen bombs, even though the combatants are prudent enough to avoid *overkill,* which might waste costly missiles on populations already dead. Compared with such neologisms, the clichés of the older armory seem tame, almost civilized; but they, too, are inhumane because they seem to celebrate organized bloodshed—or be indifferent to it—by imposing its panoply on the language of peaceful people. Thus medical injections and hard liquor are taken in *shots,* important officials are casually called *big guns* or *big shots,* salesmen reserve their *heavy artillery* as final arguments in the maneuvers of achieving sales, and various *blonde bombshells* explode seductively on the battlefields of entertainment, exposing *strategic* parts of themselves. Similarly, reporters *bombard* a public figure with insistent questions, or the *frontal assault* of inquiry may come as a *barrage* or *crossfire*, which can drive him to *diversionary tactics* or *evasive action* or to a blustering *counterattack*. Without straining reason too far, martial imagery can be applied to an efficient household—the *home front* where *reveille* comes early and everyone must *rise and shine*, usually *on the double*, and the children *pass muster* before mother scrambles the breakfast eggs according to *SOP (standing operating procedure)*. Later she will inspect her larder with *logistics* in mind and, if supplies are low, take off on *Operation Supermarket;* and all day she will remain *on active duty* until *taps*. Her husband may be *in the front line* of the legal or dental profession, working with *a corporal's guard* of assistants who help him either in *court battles* or in the *war on tooth decay*. Here follow more phrases borrowed from the language of soldiering:

about face	on the march
all-out (or *total*) war	order of the day
armed to the teeth	out of step
baptism of fire	psychological warfare
between two fires	raw recruit
bite the bullet	running fire
break ranks	show of force
brother(s) in arms	soldier of fortune
for the duration	steal a march
marching orders	task force
on the defensive (or *offensive*)	up in arms
on all fronts	war of attrition (or *of nerves*)

Minor Miracle

Cliché, the worse for posing a contradiction in terms. The noun in its weaker senses can be applied to any extraordinary quality, event or person—e.g., *a miracle of self-restraint*—but in exact usage it remains the business of God, and so far, for believers, He has not turned in a less than perfect performance. (See also MAJOR, MINOR.)

Minuscule

The correct spelling, with a *u* in the middle syllable. This is a formal word describing a style of small writing found in medieval and older manuscripts. By extension it is also applied to anything diminutive or tiny. More and more, however, it is appearing in print misspelled as *miniscule*.

Misguided Adjectives

Some writers assemble sentences like children playing at a dartboard: the throwing means more than the scoring. So with the parts of speech, and particularly with the adjective in this common misconstruction: *There has never been a more necessary time than now to begin.* The idea suffers damage because *necessary* is made to modify *time,* thus deflecting the sense of urgency from its true mark, that of making a start. The cure for such a jumble is rewording: *There has never been a time when it was more necessary* or, more simply, *It has never been more necessary.* Similarly misdirected adjectives are common in news reports, in which we meet the convict who faces *a possible life sentence* and the brawler who suffered *a possible broken nose;* even granting that anything in life is possible, *what may (possibly) be* would render the meaning of both examples in better style. From the same sources we learn of the man who died of *an apparent heart attack,* which may or may not have been apparent to others but apparently killed him, and of *apparent efforts* to achieve some goal when the efforts are manifest and only the goal is subject to speculation. And when *an approximate twenty mobsters* convene, trouble of some kind may be in the offing, but syntactical trouble is at hand. Other deflections include *the fatal scene* (can a place be implicated in homicide?), *the latest female slaying* (by or of a woman, and does murder need a gender?), *the obscene exhibition of motion pictures* (does the obscenity lie in the showing or the show?), and *the threatened highway project* that may disrupt the local ecology (what threatens what, and with what?). Certain of these journalistic usages may as well be accepted because they have acquired the semblance of idiom and little can be done to stop them anyway: *the bag of suspected heroin* and *the estimated enemy battalion,* though that marvel of cracked logic, *the attempted assassin,* must be permanently put away. Moreover, nonwriters display the same poor aim when they let fly with *an automatic winner, a positive genius,* or *a practical flood of mail,* neglecting to turn the adjectives into adverbs, and when they compile *a favorite list of people,* including *a decaffeinated drinker* or two and perhaps *a corrugated salesman.* Employers score no better when they advertise for *part-time men,* evidently seeking androgynous applicants, nor do jewelers who sell *pierced earrings.* Many misuses of this kind may get by as casual English, untidy rather than outrageous, but good writing and speaking cannot condone *an annual fifty elephants destroyed* (as if elephants died at the age of one), *an exotic dish worth sinking tentative teeth into* (as if with borrowed dentures), and *the many unnecessary lives lost in warfare* (as if any human life were surplus).

Misguided Adverbs

A sound adverbial phrase—e.g., *economically depressed areas*— can be hurled into a superlative form that makes false sense—e.g., *the most economically depressed areas,* which seems to speak of areas that are depressed in the most frugal way. Here, too, rewording is needed for clarity, sometimes by simple rearrangement *(the most depressed areas economically),* sometimes by a slight periphrasis well worth the three extra words *(the areas that are economically the most depressed).* The problem appears also in phrases cast in the comparative form: *a more technically advanced nation* should excel other nations in quibbling over its insignificant skills. A third way to misplace the adverb crops up in *so psychologically shaken*, where *so* is meant to modify *shaken* but fails in its assignment, so that the mind must try to grasp the notion of *shaken so psychologically*, whose meaning flickers like a will-o'-the-wisp. Similar examples abound, consistently exposing a blur in the writer's thought. Here are several that fail the test of clarity (compare FLOATING ADVERBS):

more culturally isolated
more intellectually stimulating
more politically active
so secretly pleased
so wickedly seductive
the most internally troubled government
the most numerically common mistakes
the most scientifically unknown realities
the most socially backward tribes

Monotonous Regularity

Cliché, used by the unoriginal with—well, monotonous regularity. Why not *persistent* or *unfailing regularity*?

More and Less

For the comparison of unequal sums or quantities, *more than* and *less than* are the clearest and most direct expressions. The alternatives *over* and *under*, *above* and *below*, *beyond* and *short of* will serve almost as well (and do serve, widely), but they have the disadvantage of striking a spark of doubt in the reader's mind, causing him to think of physical position, of a dimension of space, before he encounters the quantity. The use of *-odd* after a round number, to acknowledge a small surplus not worth specifying, will also serve if the hyphen is present to ward off ambiguity, as in *The zoo is home* *to 400-odd animals.* (But *above and beyond* and *over and above,* which seem like redundancies until they are viewed under a semantic microscope, would feel more at home with the double-word clichés listed under TWOFERS.) Two other efforts to improve on *more than* can lead the unwary writer into absurdity, as in *The airman parachuted upward of 10,000 feet to his rendezvous* and *The madman committed better than a dozen murders.* A third, *in excess of,* gives off the musty smell of formal documents; its natural domicile is the courts of law, or those reports to stockholders prepared by unsung writers. A fourth, a slang use of *plus,* may be dismissed without a qualm: *He drove at eighty-plus miles an hour* (compare SIMPLE ARITHMETIC). Finally, it is worth noting that the last four examples have no corresponding substitutes for *less than.* These would be, say, *His winnings at poker last night were downward of* or *worse than* or *in insufficiency of twenty dollars,* or *He won twenty-minus dollars;* but English in its wisdom rejects them. (See also APPROXIMATION TERMS.)

Mrs. Malaprop's Legacy

Those who know and love Mrs. Malaprop, the best-remembered character in Sheridan's *Rivals,* for her wild blunders in vocabulary, also enjoy the stumblings of her present-day apostles—or *epistles,* as she might call them. Her failing was a form of dull-eared catachresis, the confusing of words that sound almost alike, e.g., "an allegory on the banks of the Nile" (read *alligator*) or "the very pine-apple of perfection" *(pinnacle)*—puns that sound more forced than laughable today. The modern version of Mrs. Malaprop's problem differs, however, in that it does not ravage individual words but combines their meanings and implications in ludicrous ways so that they interact to generate punning ideas rather than sounds. Usually the double meaning is unconscious, as it must have been when the slogan *Lesbians, Unite!* was born. At times the humor seems deliberate, as when Latin and Greek are called *classic examples of dead languages,* or an advertisement informs us that a certain product gives a woman's legs *a whole new feel;* but we cannot be sure. Here are some random samples of such work, to be laughed at but never imitated (compare HAPHAZARD PHRASING and HAPHAZARD WORDING):

antique-finish paint that makes furniture look like new
the bare fact of giving birth
a bathroom with ample waste space
a blizzard of political hot air
a breakthrough on the sex front
the chief point about acupuncture
expanding the bottom of the economy
a freeze in the price of fresh meat
groundless objections to strip mining
the Philadelphia Eagles declared underdogs
a retired human cannonball replaced by another performer
    of the same caliber
the rocketing costs of defense
sex education considered unpalatable
a shot in the arm (i.e., money) for the drug-abuse program
uptight about constipation
virgin territory for research in obstetrics

Music Metaphors

Music, long celebrated as "the universal language of mankind," contributes many words and phrases that recur in everyday English as if they, too, were universal. They are not, or need not be. The truth is that most of them are either aged metaphors, derivative and sentimental, or borrowed musicians' shop talk—shopworn expressions that have come to *double in brass,* serving within their occupational setting and outside it, but not as well outside because they have turned into blatant clichés. Thus one form of penalty we pay for loose behavior is to *face the music,* which will impinge on our hearing as *a hell of a note* or *a sour note.* Our accusers may *pull out all the stops* when they assail our actions or else *soft-pedal* the charges, either subjecting us to *a chorus of complaints* or sounding *a responsive chord* that is *music to our ears.* Nevertheless, the critics *call the tune—the old familiar tune—harping on* or *drumming into* us the virtues that should lead us to *change our tune.* The sermonizing is a *clarion call* of exhortation, *trumpeting* the merits of the upright life. We remain unregenerate, however, refusing to *play second fiddle* in decisions affecting our conduct. From then on we *play it by ear* when pleasures beckon, *fiddling away* our time in idle dissipation; our integrity can be *bought for a song,* in particular *a siren song,* even if we provoke *a symphony of scorn* and are *drummed out* of respectable company as a result. (See also ORCHESTRATE.)

Mute Reminder of the Past

Cliché, voiced automatically by visitors to ancient monuments, such as the Parthenon and the Pyramids. Now doubly meaningless at these sites and at all the others where *son et lumière* has spread its electronic tentacles and decibels.

Nakedness Euphemisms

There is a wholesomeness in the word *naked* that is lacking in its synonymous expressions. Even *nude* sounds more formal than it should be, and certain literary phrases—*in a state of nature, in nature's garb*—imply a falsely modest blush. News reporters who use *unclad, unclothed* or *undraped* are being prissy, though they rejoice in *scantily clad,* a cliché with a built-in leer. In colloquial speech a naked person is *in the altogether, in the buff, in his birthday suit,* or *without a stitch,* and in slang he is *in the raw.* Now that exuberant young people go "streaking" (and at least one elderly couple has been reported "snailing"), it is more pointless than ever to refer to the stripped human body with averted eyes.

Nauticisms

Man's age-old love affair with the sea, whether for commerce or plunder, exerts a powerful influence on landlubbers, especially those who speak English. The result is that their language, from the purest literature on downward, is heavy with nautical terms. Poets have found the ocean a particularly fertile source to dip into for romantic–sentimental metaphors. In the nineteenth century Matthew Arnold listened gravely to its "eternal note of sadness"; Emma Willard was inspired to write *Rocked in the Cradle of the Deep;* and Longfellow apostrophized the Union in imagery as old as classical Athens: "Sail on, O Ship of State!" To this day we hear references (seldom serious) to *the bounding main, the briny deep,* and *a watery grave.* Many other seagoing expressions, however, survive in trite everyday use: in an emergency we *cut* (the anchor cable) *and run,* or on an impulse we *cut loose* (sever moorings); and, although it is a disadvantage to *miss the boat,* after we are on board it is downright hazardous to *rock the boat* because we are all *in the same boat.* Impressed by the appearance of a fellow passenger, we say that we *like the cut of his jib;* but if he turns out to be an opinionated bore we try to *take the wind out of his sails* with counterarguments or, failing, *give him a wide berth* thereafter, looking for other companions when *the coast is clear* of his presence. Terms based on a ship's deck have also drifted into landside speech: businessmen *clear the decks* to mount a new sales campaign; wage earners *hit the deck* on working days at the command of an alarm clock; baseball players wait *on deck* for their turn at bat; and it may be that on doomsday the Lord High Admiral of Creation will summon *all hands on deck* for the Judgment. Naval warfare provides a few specialized locutions for those who favor derivative language: a boxer scores a blow against his opponent *amidships;* a protest at parking regulations brings citizens to *battle stations;* a revivalist fires a *broadside* at sin; criminals find themselves on a *collision course* with the law; an epidemic of flu leaves factories without their *normal complement* of workers; an evasive official lays down a *smoke screen* to conceal the truth from investigators; and a spy *surfaces* like a submarine, visible again after a period of working in the murk. Of the nauticisms listed below, few are thoroughly at home on land, and the writer should decide which of them he can love like a seasoned sailor and which he must *steer clear of* (see also WATER METAPHORS and compare MILITARY METAPHORS):

at the helm
at sea (= bewildered)
be on (or *off*) course
be sunk (= defeated, ruined)
box the compass (= come full circle)
by dead reckoning
cast (or *drop*) anchor
double-decker (bus, sandwich, etc.)
fore and aft
get (or *lose*) one's bearings
go by the board (= overboard)
in the wake of
leeway

make headway
on an even keel
run a tight ship
set a course for
set adrift
shipshape
shove off (= leave)
stem to stern
take a new (or *a different* or *the wrong*) tack
turn turtle (= capsize)
welcome aboard
when one's ship comes in (or *home*)
with flying colors
with someone (or *something*) in tow

New Lease on Life

Cliché, an old one referring to a renewed contract between lessor and lessee (compare FOSSIL PHRASES). By now it reads like an incongruous blend of the covenants we make with earthly landlords and the uncertain span dispensed to us by the Supreme Landlord. If the phrase must be used, let it describe a second chance to attain some praiseworthy goal. A bone-dry Martini or face-lifting surgery cannot confer such benefits.

"No" Nonsense

Some champions of Purity First in English are offended by
the illogic of *post no bills,* arguing (rightly) that *post,* a direct
command, cannot be expected to act on a nonexistent *bill.*
They turn the same unforgiving eye on the mail-order commonplace *send no money* and on such a sentence as *Nobody won
the prize.* The opposite view is held with equal firmness by
those who call this disembodied usage idiomatic (it is) and
accept it without uneasiness. It is lucky for writers that they
can sidestep both the controversy and the irrational idiom;
they would hardly use the first two examples except to quote
them, and they are free to turn the third, and others like it,
into English that no reader can dispute, e.g., *None of the
contestants won the prize.*

Nonpareil Words

These form a class, chiefly of adjectives, that cannot be
preceded by *more* or *most* or by any TAKE-BACK TERM because
their meaning is absolute, allowing no comparison. One
such word is *unique,* the abused darling of Madison Avenue,
whose denizens are fond of phrases like *a most unique advance
in sprigsprocket design* or, in a tone less brash and more coy, *a
rather unique improvement in soapsudsability.* They, and others
who misuse the word, are devaluing its power to describe
something that stands unassailably alone in its category. A
collector's stamp, for example, may be *rare* or even *the rarest
of its kind,* but it cannot be *unique* unless it has no counterpart
in all philately. There are not many words of similar
strength and worth, but those that we have deserve to be
respected and conserved. Compounds beginning with *all—
an all-round athlete, an all-inclusive price*—and those built on the
Latin word for *all—an omnipresent hindrance, an omnivorous
beast*—proclaim themselves incomparable by their structure.
So do many modifiers formed with the negating syllables
im-, in-, and *un-:* nothing can be partly *immaculate, indestructible,* or *unbaptized* because the wholeness of such words cannot

be divided into degrees. It is possible, however, to limit them by *almost, nearly,* or *more nearly*—terms that acknowledge perfection to be unattainable. Thus the disputed expression in the Preamble to the Constitution, *to form a more perfect union,* long a source of pain to wordsmen, can be understood as a quest that never ends (though *a more nearly perfect union* would have precluded the quibbling); whereas *a more whole point of view,* with or without ancestral authority, must be condemned because the whole cannot be greater than itself. The list of nonpareil words grows steadily shorter as their integrity is hacked at and the mutilated pieces become replacements for more serviceable words—as, in the first example, *unique* for *unusual* or *remarkable.* Here is a selection of other unmodifiables still worth preserving:

absolute	infinite
categorical	paramount
contemporary	simultaneous
equal	supreme
essential	total
eternal	ultimate
final	unanimous
imperative	universal

Nonverbs

Turning nouns into verbs is an old habit, both good and bad, of users of the English language. The addiction took hold within a century after the Norman Conquest, as the Middle English period (roughly 1100-1500) stripped its speech of nearly all grammatical inflections and signs of gender. There was so little to distinguish a noun from a verb that the two parts of speech became easily interchangeable, and they remain nearly so to this day: to choose a colloquial but not extreme example, we have *a try* (verb to noun) at playing golf and hope *to card* (noun to verb) a good score. Not all such conversions are acceptable, however, especially the undisciplined changing of nouns to verbs. Although English today, as in the time of Shakespeare, is in an age of innovation, it also has had time to settle down with certain canons of good taste and usage, and these inspire resistance to arbitrary changes in the functions of words. But to resist is not the same as to prohibit, and discerning users of the language find nothing objectionable in many noun-verbs that have proved their worth—*to clock* a racehorse, *to document* a thesis, *to letter* a sign, *to table* a motion, and so on. The verb *to contact,* the object of anathemas when it was introduced around 1930, has won a following despite its blurry meaning. It exemplifies a class of noun-verbs that spring into vogue and find an irrational welcome. Others like it are considered here, of which some will die presently and some will live for a period no one can measure, perhaps as long as the language is spoken. The writer's responsibility is to accept the specimens that seem right to him and to others of equal perceptiveness, and always to reject those that serve no purpose.

Of noun-verbs related to *contact,* for instance, most needs are filled by *to cable, phone, signal,* and *wire* (and now, inevitably, *to satellite*), but the newer *to long-distance* and *to message* stand out as idiocies. Financing is covered by *to bankroll* for the flippant, *to fund* for the affluent, and *to expense* for the uncouth. The complexities of modern transportation almost force us *to bus* schoolchildren, *to cab* or *helicopter* to the office and *to jet* across greater distances. The grimmer complexities of warfare have dictated *to bomb, to shell, to torpedo,* and recently *to napalm,* along with *to cease-fire,* a zany verb formed from a verbal phrase composed to serve as a noun. Radio and television have given us *to air,* which prompts the thought of dirty linen, *to anchor, to network,* and such unleavened verbs as *to guest, to host, to guest-host, to guest-star* and *to sub-host.* If newspaper editors choose *to by-line* a news account and *to front-page* it, that is their jargonistic right, but when the hangers-on of publishing sink so low as *to author* a book, *to biograph* a public figure, *to critique* a play, *to ghost* a speech, and *to script* a scenario, they subvert the dignity of writing. Perhaps the worst noun-to-verb indignities are committed in the occupations known collectively as Broadway, where make-believe prevails even in speech; this is, or may as well have been, the birthplace of *to debut, to duet, to emcee* (in full, *to master-of-ceremonies*) and its monstrous mate *to femcee, to encore, to prelude,* and *to première* (whose antonym, in a quip attributed to Jacques Barzun, must be *to derrière*).

Some of the verbs noted here may already command, or will command before long, full or partial respect in good English. The likeliest exception is *to jawbone,* the current political slang for the act of persuading the reluctant; until the Old Testament is read no more, the noun will always bring to mind Samson's feat of slaying a thousand men with "a fresh jawbone of an ass." Among the miscellaneous nonverbs that follow, the entries are authentic nouns but still deplorable as verbs; the intended objects are provided for some, but all are to be read as infinitives, preceded by an imaginary *to* (compare BACK FORMATIONS):

birth (a baby)
gift
houseguest (intransitive)
housewife (intransitive)
loan (books, money, etc.)
maximum (of an automo-
  bile's highest speed)
motion (for adjournment)

nutshell (a long story)
opinion (an opinion)
parent
river (tears)
signature
springboard (a proposal)
suicide (intransitive)
watchdog (the treasury)

Not That, Not Too

These devices of negation need careful scrutiny before they can be included in good writing.

1. *Not that,* with *that,* an adverb meaning *so* or *to that extent,* has only recently moved upward from its place among colloquialisms: *The choreography was not that clever; His predictions are*

never that accurate. When, however, the context points to a comparison but fails to draw one, the usage should be abandoned for clearer phrasing: for *Popular tunes are not that good nowadays* write *not as good as they once were* or omit *that.* A common longer version, as in *The players' scores are not all that far apart,* appears to gain strength from the emphatic *all* but does not dispose of the shortcomings inherent in the plain *not that,* and despite its growing acceptance it still does not seem ready for formal use.

2. *Not too,* meaning *not very,* is better established in the language but has less logic in its favor. Since *very* connotes a large amount and *too* an excess, they cannot be interchanged in a sentence without damage to its sense, and yet *not too* is often encountered where *not very* is meant. The explanation lies in a rhetorical figure known as litotes, a form of verbal acrobatics that tempers an assertion by denying the contrary, as in *not without merit.* (The most frequently quoted instance is "a citizen of no mean city"—the words by which St. Paul described himself in *The Acts of the Apostles.*) Accordingly, *eyesight that is not too keen* may be taken as a polite understatement and *not too eager for marriage* as simple reticence, though the extenuating *too* can be left out in both examples to make them stronger and, as arrangements of interdependent words, more reasonable. The real danger in *not too* is that of ambiguity: if a book is *not too proper for summer reading,* is its theme or style inappropriately ponderous or its content just racy enough? Such questions, once raised or perceived, can be resolved only by revision.

Nouns as Modifiers

Putting nouns to use as adjectives is a historic mechanism in English (compare NONVERBS) and one source of its richness and pliancy as a medium of conveying thought. The variety achieved by this usage is evident in many consolidated compounds—*breadbasket, gasworks, postmaster*—and in the far more numerous separated pairs—*glass pitcher, opium den, woman lawyer.* This flexibility is not unlimited, however; too much reliance on its convenience can lead to boring prose and spectacular ambiguity. In the phrase *child bride,* for example, the sense of the modifying noun is unmistakable, but the same noun made part of another combination can yield more than one interpretation: is a *child murderer* a villain who kills children or a tot with a knack for dispatching his playmates and his elders? And does *burglary protection* work to the advantage of the burglar or his victim? That this kind of quibbling can be overdone is evident in *drug rehabilitation program,* for example, which only a willful sophist will read as *a program to rehabilitate drugs,* though his misinterpretation is implicit in the elliptical phrase. But sometimes the boredom and the ambiguity collaborate to baffle the reader, as in *drug abuse pioneer,* which can be clarified only by rearranging its elements and adding essential words: *a pioneer in methods of controlling drug abuse.* A similar reconstruction can change the terse obscurity of *Baptist Elderly Home* to the more relaxed *Baptist Home for the Elderly,* if denomination is not a criterion of admission, or *Home for Elderly Baptists* if it is. The massing of noun-adjectives before the noun they modify is common in graceless news writing: *deposed Nonstop Transportation Company assistant vice-president in charge of operations Arthur Jimsonweed* crams needed information into the wrong place, and *the no load $25 million in assets New York based growth oriented mutual fund* makes the same ineptness worse by its naked lack of punctuation. Educators should be keenly alert to the requirements of clarity but plod along under self-inflicted REDUNDANCIES like *guidance counselor* and absurdities like *hearing handicapped teacher.* Here are a few other stultified locutions used by teachers:

Cerebral Palsy Preschool Development Program (a program to develop cerebral palsy in preschool children?)
Early Childhood Certification (the licensing of infants to teach?)

Learning Disabilities Instructor (someone to instill disabilities in learning?)
Mentally Retarded Teacher (a pointed paradox?)

Now

This clear monosyllabic adverb is to be preferred wherever possible over the drawn-out phrasing of *at present, at the moment, at this hour, point,* or *juncture,* and, the wordiest of all, *at the present time.* In some instances the longer synonym can improve rhythm or euphony: at the end of a secretary's standard line, "Mr. Smith is in conference," *now* sounds more abrupt than *at the moment,* although *just now* or *right now* would serve less formally. If she says *at this point in time,* she is imitating wasteful LEGAL LINGO, and if she says *in this time frame,* only a language-mauler from the Washington bureaucracy would understand her. Those who retain *now* but, fearing that it is too lean, fatten it into *as of now* are adding worthless blubber—*The train leaves (as of) now*—and the corpulence grows even more unsightly in *as of this instant, hour, minute, moment,* or *time.* Among other ways of specifying the present, *currently* is useful in extending the idea of *now* over a longer period, as in *currently writing a book;* but *presently,* which began by meaning "at once" and then settled into the less urgent sense of "before long," becomes both odd and ambiguous when forced to mean *now: the orator presently speaking* may be halfway through his discourse or still waiting to mount the podium. The adjectival *now,* common in the language for centuries as a temporal modifier—e.g., *the now king* (compare *the then king*)—has been turned in our time into a faddish neologism for "contemporary" or "ultramodern"— e.g., *the now courses in college* or *the now swimsuits*—a usage to be avoided and, as soon as better thought prevails, to be banished. It is important in writing to respect the simple meaning of the present tense, which confers contemporaneity by definition and seldom needs the prop of *now* or its equivalents except for emphasis or to convey a nuance: *a study that is now under way* is merely under way.

Null Sounds

The meaningless noises we make as a preliminary to speaking—*ah, er, uh, um, ahem,* or simply the drawing in and letting out of an audible breath—help prolong the comfort of silence before our words commit us to a statement or opinion that we fear we may regret. Along with these nonwords, two real words—*well* and *why*—serve the same procrastinating purpose when they function without meaning in answers to questions: *Well, I remember thinking it was a strange explanation; Why, he was here just a minute ago.* The adverb *now* amounts to another nullity when it attempts to emphasize—*Now stop that*—or when it encumbers a resumptive phrase—*Now, as I was saying.* . . . Likewise, in slang, the use of *man* as an interjection reduces the word to a useless grunt; a fondness for *like* as a senseless expletive—*On Saturday nights we, like, go to the movies*—amounts to a neurotic verbal tic, as does the interpolation of *I mean* where the meaning is already clear. And the more widespread habit of ending a declarative sentence with an unnecessary question—*Get my point? O.K.? Right? Understand?*—betrays severe self-doubt. Even the normal interjection *oh,* when not expressing true surprise or indignation (e.g., *Oh, how cruel!*), can postpone an answer or admission briefly: *Oh, I did have a couple of drinks.* All such gropings for reprieve or forgiveness belong in casual speech only; in writing they look silly except when quoted, and even then can seem unnatural. (See also YOU KNOW.)

Omnibus Nouns

Considered as vehicles of communication, some nouns have room only for the driver, some admit a small number of passengers, and a few resemble a large, lumbering bus during the rush hour, crowded with nondescript riders, or meanings. The more meanings a word can encompass, the less precise and clear it is.

1. *Jumbo Buses.* Today one of the most prevalent omnibus words—and one of the hollowest and most pompous—is *aspect,* a demonstrably bad choice in these examples: *the health-giving aspects of wine (properties* or *qualities*); *the irksome aspects of a job* (long hours, heavy responsibilities, etc.); *the military aspect of the war* (shooting, bombing, etc.); *the managerial aspect of sports* (management). Equally diffuse and inadequate is *factor* in its many usurpations and pointless intrusions: *the age factor in dismissals* (age as a reason for); *a decision determined by many factors* (considerations); *the danger factor in smoking cigarettes* (omit factor); *a disparity caused by many factors* (due to many causes). (The boss who predicts that sales will increase by *a factor of two* is not using an omnibus word; he is trying to say that sales will double but has forgotten how. Compare SIMPLE ARITHMETIC.)

2. *Empty Buses.* Colloquial usage calls on certain other words to serve in all-encompassing senses, to the neglect of sharper and more literate choices: *Caviar is an expensive affair* (food? luxury?); *Fallen arches are a painful business* (condition? affliction?); *Hate is a corrosive proposition* (emotion? feeling?).

3. *Minibuses.* A few other nouns may be classified as minibuses, which take on enough figurative uses to become fashionable among the addicts of novelty but stop short of becoming mass carriers of meanings. One such word is *concept,* which should be reserved for man's noblest theorizing about spirit and matter but is reduced to meaning little more than an idea or proposal in *the concept of making marijuana legal, of reducing taxes,* or *of United States defense in the Mediterranean.* Another is *context,* now lifted out of its literal sense, of the words before and after a written passage that help to clarify it, and put to work supplying the foggy "surrounding circumstances" in *the context of China's social system, of life in a kibbutz,* or *of solving crossword puzzles.*

4. *Wayward Buses.* All the preceding vehicles are dwarfed by the supercapacious constructions of slang: *gadget* is perhaps the best known in a lunatic list that includes *dingus, doodad, doohickey, doojigger, gizmo, widget,* and, in another wing of the asylum, *thingamabob, thingamajig, thingamananny, thingummy, whatchamacallit,* and *whatzis.* Normally, these designate people or objects too insignificant to name, or to remember the names of—witness Mr. Whozis, who swore he would never forget Miss What's-Her-Name.

On Pins and Needles

Cliché, based on the tingling in an arm or leg that is "asleep" and has begun to waken from its numbness. By extension the phrase connotes a helpless uneasiness, such as an expectant father feels outside the delivery room. When his suspense and agony reach their sharpest, he is said to be *on tenterhooks*—a cruel metaphor derived from the rows of bent prongs on the tenters or racks once used for stretching cloth to dry. Both clichés, like the sensations they stand for, are best avoided.

On the Spur of the Moment

Cliché, a figure of speech for unpremeditated action. Dating from the early nineteenth century, long before the internal combustion engine was invented, the phrase turns a person into a metaphorical horse with a skittish rider on its back.

One-Way Words

Elevators not only elevate their passengers to upper floors but take them down again. Escalators help people to ascend *and* descend, though their name goes back to the old military escalade, the use of ladders in the scaling of ramparts. These two usages, which primarily express upward movement, illustrate the ability of certain one-way words to encompass their own reversal, doubling their meanings without creating a noticeable confusion in the mind. However, a much more regrettable semantic change takes place when two-way words, or radial words that can, with the help of modifiers, swing through an entire circle of connotations, are brought to rest pointing in a single direction, like compass needles, deprived of the freedom to move. The writers and speakers responsible for this wastefulness are fond of saying that inflation or prices are *spiraling* (up or down?) instead of *increasing* or *rising*—verbs that carry the true sense by pointing unmistakably upward. It also pleases them to think that *a fraction* (or *a percentage*) denotes a small part, although 999/1000 is still a fraction of the whole, and that *an indefinite period* denotes a long time, although the phrase can stretch from microseconds to eons. The young man who thinks of his girl as *different* is equally guilty of one-way semantics; and his case grows worse if he praises her as *something* or *something else again*. Still other words become fixed in an unqualified connotation of "good" when they should be free to express the opposite as well:

a car that *performs* can perform well or badly
gas-station *service* sometimes becomes disservice
a man of *taste* may wallow in the hideous
quality education leaves the quality uncertain
a reading *experience* could be one that induces retching
a student who *achieves* may achieve only a police record

Optical Delusions

If *the hand is quicker than the eye,* as good magicians know, then *seeing* is not always *believing,* despite the purveyors of folk wisdom. Nevertheless, many writers remain fond of certain words related to vision even if they do not help the reader to see and often blur his understanding. These are fashionable words, used and overused in figurative senses until, like the crazy mirrors in amusement parks, they reflect distorted images. Fastidious writers should *take a dim view* of the inflated or inappropriate meanings flaunted by the following:

1. *Focus.* Any boy playing with a magnifying glass learns that it can bend the rays of light to make them converge at a single point. In time, after mastering the lenses of cameras and microscopes, he may make a metaphor of the physical phenomenon, learning to *focus attention* or *energy* on the work, before him. Beyond this sense of concentration, however, the word cannot be pushed without becoming indistinct. It is intelligible to speak of *the focus of an inquiry* but not of *an overwhelming focus on personalities,* which equips the noun with an ill-advised attribute. In *Football is the focus of a national debate, focus* is misused for *subject,* and in *The heroin traffic has shifted its focus to Southeast Asia* the preferable word may be *base* or *operations,* but no one can be sure because the writer was not.

2. *Image.* Another good word led astray, but by cynics rather than fumbling faddists. In its present use, as the popular view or opinion of a prominent person or institution, or even of a brand of dried prunes, the term is not only superficial but very often meretricious because it carries the implication that the view can be changed by clever manipulation of the public's emotions. The words attributed to God in *Genesis,* "Let us make man in our image, after our likeness," show an honest, realistic use of *image;* but in today's image-making the purpose (seldom denied) is to implant a dreamy, unexamined approbation in the minds of others, even if what they are made to approve of is a mirage.

3. *Pattern.* From its visual sense of design, *pattern* lends itself to overuse as a metaphor. It tends to take on meanings better expressed in other ways, and its popularity becomes an impediment to clear writing. Action that takes place repeatedly without noteworthy change falls easily into a *pattern—the chills-and-fever pattern of malaria, the social pattern of the bee-*

hive—but the doings of people, being less predictable, do not submit to such facile regimentation: *the American pattern of drug abuse* obscures the idea of *habit* or *manner,* and *the religious pattern of life* assumes an unattainable uniformity among believers, whereas the unpatterned *religious life* leaves room for anyone drawn to it.

4. *Picture.* Long before the blessings of the television *picture* shone forth, this word had found a place in certain fixed expressions: a girl might be said to be *as pretty as a picture,* one twin *the picture* of the other, and a man *the picture of health;* and, since about 1920, people or circumstances might be *in* (or *out of*) *the picture,* a vague complex of elements making up a particular subject, such as a crime and the suspects involved in it. Now, however, probably emboldened by its antics on the cathode tube, *picture* has come into pandemic use as a tuft of padding that may mean "outlook" or "prospect" or nothing definable: *the Federal budget picture, the automobile industry's profit picture, tomorrow's weather picture.* For the *mixed picture* revealed in, say, a nationwide poll, we must postulate an inept cameraman and a double or multiple exposure.

5. *Profile.* In its overblown uses, *profile* is a young rival of *picture* and may overtake it soon. It is now fashionable to speak of *the profile of a space mission* (its program), *the profile of the stock market* (*its chart* or *performance*), or, with supreme vagueness, *the profile of a Federal program* (its efficiency? goal? organization?). In scientific extensions, the word is soundly used as a summary of data: to a mapmaker, *the profile of a range of hills;* to a physician, *the biochemical profile of a patient;* and so on. But in *low profile,* a phrase-craze of the moment, the figurative use transcends its rational limits when it is misused for "inconspicuous," as in *low-profile animals endowed with protective coloration,* or for "unobtrusive," as in *the low-profile tactics of a pickpocket.* No doubt the language will outgrow this mannerism, as it outgrew other visual metaphors—the doughty leader who once *stood out in bold relief,* for example, and the *thumbnail sketch* that came into favor at the beginning of this century. The pictorial term *vignette,* for a

short, delicate piece of writing, seems also to be fading, but *silhouette,* as in *the small silhouette of an emerging nation,* is borrowing fraternal strength from the abuse of *profile,* and will bear watching by clear-eyed antifaddists.

Or Anything, or Something

These phrases, sometimes followed by *like that,* hover between ETCETERAS and NULL SOUNDS in popular speech, adding words but no ideas to what has been said: *I wasn't asleep or anything; He thinks he's a prince or something.* The usage finds some validity in the old distinction between a bachelor girl (she never married) and a spinster (she never married or anything), but elsewhere it is a witless bad habit, like clearing the throat or cracking the knuckles.

Orchestrate

A recent favorite with faddists, who use it as a smart MUSIC METAPHOR to replace many worthier verbs: a corporation *orchestrates* its influence on government officials (*exerts* or *manipulates*); a novelist *orchestrates* his plot (*creates* or *constructs*); and before long a gifted mechanic may *orchestrate* an engine instead of giving it a tune-up.

Overall

If *overall* appeared on this page for the last time, never to reappear elsewhere, the language would be well served. As adjective and adverb, the word contributes nothing but monotony to current prose, where it presumes to replace other and better expressions of totality—*the overall budget* (total), *his overall manner* (general), *a successful stratagem overall* (as a whole)—and crashes in where it is not, or should not be, invited—*the overall consumption of aspirin this year, the overall importance of Columbus's discoveries, the overall ramifications of the plot to kill Cock Robin.* If, along with these tiresome uses, we also lost the valid ones—e.g., *the overall length of a dinosaur,* including its tail—the gain would still outweigh the loss. Should all the *overalls* in use today wind up in Mrs. Murphy's chowder, only her reputation as a cook would suffer. (Compare ALL ABOUT ALL.)

Overwhelming Majority

Cliché, at its worst when not based on a credible census or poll. A *majority* estimated as *great* or *vast* sounds equally hackneyed and unconvincing without statistics to support it, especially when all that needs to be said is *most people* or *nearly everyone.* If anybody speaks of an *overwhelming minority,* ignore him. (Compare APPROXIMATION TERMS.)

Partly and Partially

Whether a glass is *partly* or *partially* filled with water is not an important question, except that the first adverb is shorter and therefore preferable, and the second is longer and therefore more attractive to the devotees of elongation. There is a more refined distinction to be drawn between the two words. The difference is delicate but worth the writer's attention. A *part,* being a piece of the whole, can be considered either by itself, as a separate entity, or in relation to the larger parent entity. When we concentrate on the *part* rather than the whole, the correct adverb is *partly,* as in *ore that is partly iron;* when we think of the aggregate as incomplete, with some part missing, we can use *partially,* as in *hospital costs partially covered by insurance.* This rule of usage is not inexorable, and the writer can follow it *partly* or *partially,* but the better choice is nearly always *partly.*

People, Places, and Things

Cliché, a blowzy sweetheart of the news media. The phrase, promising varied delights, rivals the older *here, there, and everywhere* in comprehensive scope—and in overstatement.

Pet Peeve

Cliché, rooted in slang. Like its cousins, *pet aversion* and *pet hate*, it suggests a spoiled foot-stamping child.

Phony Context

Texts on English composition emphasize the need of a vague quality called coherence. It is not enough, they explain, that every sentence in a theme should stick to the main subject (that is the concern of unity, another devil that besets the writer); it must also stick to, or cohere with, the sentences before and after it, so that the reader can discern the logic that connects the series. A student who writes, *"The boy has a reputation for being wild. But Tony has a kind heart,"* will be corrected promptly by his teacher. A troubled mother who writes to an advice-dispensing columnist, *"My daughter just received her second divorce. Alice loves to go to parties,"* will probably not be corrected, and the reader will wonder whether Alice is the only woman in the domestic drama or a second one abruptly added to the cast of characters. This is unhinged writing, almost forgivable in the learner and the amateur but not in the professional journalist, who often ignores coherence by filing a report based on this model:

"A man lost his right leg last night in a shoe store during a dispute with the proprietor.
"John Johns was rushed to the hospital. . . ."

If the reporter is asked whether John Johns is the proprietor or the injured man, he will argue that the "context" excludes the proprietor even though the un-coherent account does not. He could just as easily have written, *"The victim, John Johns . . ."* and earned an A in composition and a vote of gratitude from his readers.

Play with Dynamite

Cliché, warning the careless of explosive consequences implicit in their behavior; akin to *play with fire,* a game for reckless sports who *play around* or *play fast and loose,* risking the blisters caused by scandal. The burns are equally painful to the unscrupulous who set out to *play both ends against the middle* but often *play into the hands* of the adversary instead.

Playing-card Metaphors

The phrase *according to Hoyle* invokes an ultimate authority as impeccable in his pronouncements as Dear Abby and Amy Vanderbilt are in theirs. Hoyle's specialty was games of skill, principally card games, but some persons have never learned this, and they do not hesitate to tell us of a judge whose rulings in court are invariably *according to Hoyle,* or of an engaged couple who conducted their entire courtship *according to Hoyle.* Considering that Edmond Hoyle, an English lawyer turned card expert, flourished more than two centuries ago, it is understandable that the kind of rules he laid down should become blurred at last in vernacular usage; but the phrase itself, one of the hardiest clichés ever devised, is seldom misused by card players, and it does symbolize the rampant permeation of our language by metaphors based on this ancient pastime. From the tenuous validity of fortunetelling, we surmise whether success, our own or another's, is or is not *in the cards.* If we are careless in arranging our plans, we construct a flimsy *house of cards.* But we applaud an amateur wit or clown as *a card,* honor almost any expert as *an ace* (a fighter pilot in the First World War, a bricklayer, and, by extreme extension, a diplomat or a gynecologist), and use *joker* to belittle any man, especially a know-it-all, and to expose sly wording in laws and documents that nullifies their apparent purpose. Cheating at cards has created its own small lexicon of commonplace phrases: the *cardsharp* deals *from the bottom of the deck, with a cold deck* (concealed on his person), *with a stacked deck,* or *without a full deck,* or he may execute a *fast shuffle* in which one or more valuable cards are *lost in the shuffle*—not counting that foresighted *ace up his sleeve.* Honest players keep their hands *aboveboard* where the others can observe them, and, when candor requires, *lay their cards on the table.* He who *plays his cards right,* bringing his *trump card* into action opportunely without first *tipping his hand,* will avoid having to *chuck, toss,* or *throw in his hand* and thus will not find himself *in the hole* (his loss recorded by a circle drawn around the amount). Other general terms contributed by card-playing to everyday English include the *ante,* which partners *chip in* when they go into business together, and the *blue-chip* securities they hope to accumulate. If they quarrel, one may express his anger *in spades,* demanding a *Fair Deal* (Harry Truman's slogan), a *New Deal* (Franklin Roosevelt's, but used earlier by Mark Train and others), or a *Square Deal* (Theodore Roosevelt's, incorporating a favorite VAGUE ADJECTIVE of his day).

Hundreds of formal games and variations have been invented for the standard fifty-two-card deck—among them Klabberjass, Slobberhannes, and Snip Snap Snorem—but few have spread their terminology beyond the card table. From cribbage we inherit the FOSSIL PHRASE *to leave in the lurch; euchre,* used as a verb, gives us a slangy synonym for to outwit or outmaneuver, and the chin-up expression *to go it alone;* and faro adds *to call the turn* (to guess in what order the last three cards will be exposed). Bridge provides more terms, though some are proper to other games as well: *finesse, follow suit, grand slam, one's long* (or *short*) *suit, squeeze play.* But poker ranks as the most prolific of all, spattering the language with the cant of hard-bitten gamblers. Two of their expressions have attained an independent life and meaning: *to pass the buck,* originally a rejection of one's turn to deal, now stands for any shirking of responsibility; and *back to back,* used with precision in stud poker when a player's first two cards are a pair, one dealt face down and the next face up, has gone on a wild migration toward the sense of consecutive, as in *back-to-back home runs* by a baseball team and possibly, unless reason intercedes in time, the *back-to-back husbands* of a twice-married woman. The remaining pokerisms, clinging closer to their origin, need no elucidation for the initiate, but their overuse in figurative writing by tyros, whether for color or vigor or out of want of originality, must be challenged as a misdeal (see also GAMBLING METAPHORS):

ace in the hole	penny-ante (= trivial)
ace-high	play one's cards close to the
call one's bluff	chest
four-flusher	poker face
kitty	showdown
openers	stand pat
pat hand	two (or *three*) of a kind

Portmanteau Words

"You see, it's like a portmanteau—there are two meanings packed up into one word." With this explanation in *Through the Looking-Glass,* Lewis Carroll gave a name to his coinages of two-in-one nonsense words, few of which have found their way into ordinary English. Today we recognize his *chortle* and *snark*—the first apparently a blend of *chuckle* and *snort,* the second of *snake* and *shark*—but have forgotten what he meant by *mimsy* (*miserable* and *flimsy*) and *slithy* (*slimy* and *lithe*). Word-makers were performing the telescoping trick long before Carroll, and some of them produced clearer and more durable combinations: *tragicomedy* appeared in the sixteenth century and *dumfound* (from *dumb* and *confound*) in the seventeenth; *anecdotage,* as a pun about old people who spin out long reminiscences, was in use three decades before Alice set foot in Wonderland (compare LUNCH). By now we have accepted *happenstance* as a colloquialism, and those who favor *guesstimate* may live to see it raised up out of slang; but *irregardless* (from *irrespective* and *regardless*) must molder in blithering illiteracy for all time. Like the poets who compose dirty limericks, the creators of cross-pollinated words are usually anonymous, though *globaloney* is explicitly attributed to Clare Boothe Luce and crudities like *infanticipate* and *splituation* were once welcomed from Walter Winchell and even hailed as wit. What merchants and their hired hucksters have done with this flexible device need not occupy us here (see MANGLED GREEK WORDS), but certain clusters of routine weldings are worth a quick appraisal. Travel by car gave us the inevitable *motel* for *motor hotel* (*cartel* means something else), and the popularity of boating went on to burden us, unofficially so far, with *boatel* and *floatel.* Our weather experts accepted *smog,* for *smoke* and *fog,* as early as 1926, and its offspring, *smaze,* for *smoke* and *haze,* is now a legitimate dictionary entry, but its newest baby, *snizzle,* for *snow* and *drizzle,* must be greeted with *"Gesundheit"* each time it sprays the air. Current social problems have inspired such nonce or nonsense terms as *Nixonomics, parochaid,* and *stagflation* to try the souls of lexicographers, who must also cope with the lunacy of *superette,* a food market that is large and little at the same time, and with the rabid minds that planned a *sno-fari* to hunt wolves by snowmobile in Canada (they were forbidden). The final cluster is a mass of juvenile puns built on *sex* and its phonetic similarity to the prefix *ex: sexperiment, sexpert,* and *sexploit* are among those current, and may *sextermination* overtake the lot. Except for serious and useful blends that name something new—*television* serves well as an example— the making of portmanteau words is only a game that amuses children briefly, as Lewis Carroll must have known. Most such hybrids are born in delicate health and, let us hope, soon expire—as some of the following have had the grace to do already:

alcoholocaust
beautility
benefactory
bookritic
broasted
fantabulous
filmusical
frailment
insinnuendo
numbody
popollution

shamateur
shemale
slanguage
slimnastics
snoopervise
superific
swellegant
swingles
telescoop
tripewriter

Posture

Starting with the basic sense of how a person carries his body (with *good* or *bad posture*), this word has undergone a natural growth toward the abstractions of *attitude,* as in *a hostile posture,* and of *position* or *stand,* as in *a surgeon's posture on abortion.* More vaguely, the word has been extended to cover groups of circumstances, as in *the present posture of inter-American relations.* From this borderline application, *posture* has been stretched beyond the reach of its roots, and their ability to nourish it, by being elevated to smart uses and misuses. We can be thankful (but how long?) that it has not yet invaded the premises belonging to *inclination* and *predisposition,* which are served by stalwart alternates like *bent* and *bias,* and by upstart expressions like *psychological set*—e.g., against waking up early—and, more recently in government, by a *tilt* toward one side or another in an international squabble, as if foreign affairs reminded our officials of pinball machines. But *posture* may still turn up in these senses because it has become a fad word, permeating the airwaves and the printed page and thereby winning a priority in sluggish minds. It has already appeared as a DRONE WORD in *a corporation's earnings (posture)*, as a poor substitute for *policy* in *the Federal Reserve's tight-credit posture*, and as flabby nonsense in *the glut posture of the job market*. In a final, hardly believable distortion—*A man charged with rape loses a tremendous amount of posture in the community*—this muddied word, by some subterranean confluence of meanings, washes out *prestige, reputation, stature*, and even the *face* that stiff-necked people take great pains to *save*.

Pregnancy Euphemisms

By now the forthright word for impending motherhood has become acceptable in speech and print, but many of its substitutes persist wherever Victorian prudery prevails. A few of the old simperings about gestation have disappeared—that a woman is *in a certain, delicate* or *interesting condition*, or, with Gallic subtlety borrowed from Late Latin, that she is *enceinte* (ungirdled). Certain homelier terms are current as colloquialisms—that she is *anticipating, expecting*, or *in the family way*, or that she is harboring a tenant *in the oven* (compare BLESSED EVENT). Although there is a simple dignity in being *with child* or about to *become a mother*, other efforts to avoid *pregnant* imply an unseemly shame at having to admit an act of copulation. In slang this taboo, like all others, is treated with rowdy defiance: in the United States a pregnant woman has been *knocked up;* in Britain, she has been *shot in the giblets*.

Prolong the Agony

Cliché, the demotic phrase for masochism—the psychological kind rather than the physical or sexual. Healthy English, like the healthy writer, abhors the self-torment of hand-me-down expressions.

Provincial Wit

The English language is richly provided with one-sentence and one-phrase jokes, most of which were current before the twentieth century. That they are still in use is proof of their vitality. Some are crude and lusty, like the frontiersmen who made them up. Others reflect the settled life of small towns and the homely humor of an earlier day. Everyone recognizes them instantly, but whether with a smile or a shudder depends on one's feeling about hackneyed imagery. Certain SIMILES WITH AS have lost the sparkle they once had: *as busy as a one-armed paperhanger, as easy as falling off a log, as slow as molasses in January.* So has someone with *an ax to grind, a bone to pick,* or *a chip on his shoulder,* and his antithesis who *would give you the shirt off his back* and *wouldn't hurt a fly.* And so has everyone else who seeks to entertain with similar banalities. If a man *cut his eyeteeth* on life's hardships, to become the smartest fellow *in captivity,* with *no flies on him,* he still might *spill the beans* in some unguarded moment or *let the cat out of the bag*—perhaps the same chop-licking *cat that ate the canary* but failed to *get his tongue* while it was wagging. This man's wife may be *a millstone around his neck* and, if *she is no better than she should be,* may *pull the wool over his eyes.* His mood varies daily: one morning he wakes up *bright-eyed and bushy-tailed, raring to go,* but the next he *gets up on the wrong side of the bed,* ready to *fly off the handle.* Going out in a cloudburst, he observes that it is *raining pitchforks* or *cats and dogs,* or *coming down in buckets,* a meteorological condition that creates *nice weather for ducks. Once in a blue moon* he runs into a friend he has not seen *in a coon's age* or *a month of Sundays* or meets a stranger whom, until that moment, *he did not know from Adam.* They start drinking *to beat the band,* decide to *paint the town red,* and finish by *making a spectacle of themselves,* each man standing there *with egg on his face.* . . . The parable does not end there, *not by a jugful,* but the moral is already overdue: a writer who relies on provincialisms to enliven his style will *paint himself into a corner,* and P.D.Q.—*no two ways about it.* (See also CRACKER-BARREL TERMS, SIMILES WITH LIKE, and VILLAGE IDIOMS.)

Here is a further sampling from our heritage of once-vivid wit:

a drop in the bucket
a sight for sore eyes
at the drop of a hat
can hardly hear oneself
  think
caught with one's pants
  down
come out in the wash
do a land-office business
everything but the kitchen
  sink
fight one's way out of a paper bag
go off half-cocked
keep banker's hours
knock over with a feather
laugh on the other side of
  one's face

lead the life of Riley
make the fur (or *feathers* or
  sparks) fly
more (of something) than
  one can shake a stick at
more than one way to skin
  a cat
not born yesterday
paddle one's own canoe
swallow the dictionary
swear a blue streak
sweep under the rug
talk through one's hat
throw a monkey wrench
  into the works
walking encyclopedia
whistle in the dark

Provisional Opinions

A good way to eviscerate a statement is to express it as an opinion rather than a fact or a truth. This kind of diffidence becomes philosophers and other delvers who understand the limitations of their knowledge—as Tennyson wrote, "Believing where we cannot prove"—but only a Milquetoast mind will lead its owner to say *I believe it snowed last night* when he sees his neighbor shoveling out his driveway. It is fair to hedge when what is said demands the restraint of *maybe: I consider him a liar* tempers an accusation that still lacks proof, but *He is a liar* permits no doubt. Thus the following phrases have their proper uses, but they must not be permitted to

hamper forthright speech (see also NULL SOUNDS and TAKE-
BACK TERMS):

as (or *so*) far as I know
as I understand it (or *the
facts*)
I am convinced (or *of the
opinion* or *persuaded*)
I feel (or *assume, presume,* or
think)
I have no doubt
I have the (or *an*) impression

in my estimation (or *judgment, opinion,* or *view*)
I take it
it seems to me
it strikes me that
my information is
to (the best of) my knowledge
to my way of thinking

Pseudoscience

Our language reflects what we consider important, and the
importance of science in modern life puts us at ease with
words that should never have escaped from the laboratory.
We say *detergent* instead of soap substitute, *insecticide* instead
of bug killer, and *transistor* (short for transistorized radio) as if
we understood the principles of solid-state semiconductors.
But this sort of borrowing does no serious harm after the
neologisms have become established, as some of our older
scientisms prove. It is all right, for example, for a young
woman to *gravitate* toward a man of *magnetic personality* who
electrifies her by his charm and *galvanizes* her soul, probably
because he is (more colloquially) a *live wire*. It is less acceptable, because more pompous, for her to try to give the new
relationship *impetus* or *momentum* too soon. And it is lament-
able taste, after she knows him better, if she falls back on the
more arid metaphors of physics by saying that he *fills a
vacuum* in her life despite his *low boiling point* and tendency to
follow the path of least resistance (as lightning does) in letting his
temper flash forth, and his readiness to *polarize* those about
him because he has no perception of the *statics and dynamics* of

human emotions, being impervious to all *vibrations*. The same young woman can characterize the end of the romance in clichés from other branches of science. She can explain that what seemed to be *the right chemistry* between them, seeping through their affections *by osmosis*, went wrong when he began pursuing an unmaidenly wench, the *catalyst* of the breakup who caused him to fail *the acid test* of fidelity. In time the jilted one, shifting to metaphors of space, may look back fondly on the hours she spent *in orbit* with him, exchanging kisses in *astronomical* numbers and soaring aloft to *stratospheric* ecstasy.

The *thrust* of all this (to borrow a word as old as SWORDPLAY and spearwork but now, on the analogy of the fiery gases shooting out of the bottom of a spacecraft, enjoying rejuvenation as a voguish replacement for "purpose" or "main point") is that the newer scientific terms stand out obtrusively when they appear as metaphors in otherwise good writing. It is affected—and farfetched—to say that a gathering mob grew to the *critical mass* that touched off a riot, and that the violence spread by *chain reaction* until a *fallout* of squad cars arrived and restored calm. And it is a silly byplay of computer jargon to speak of porpoises *programed* (rather than trained) to deposit dirty-trick devices in enemy waters. A worker may announce at quitting time—with a wink and a wetting of his lips—that he is *programed* for a double Scotch, but he does not pretend to have such matters *down to a science*. (See also IMPACT and compare LOWER MATHEMATICS.)

Push-Pull Expressions

These are used chiefly by writers on financial subjects who count well but have no sense of the obtuseness of reverse English, a stylistic fault that yanks the reader first one way and then another. One of our Presidents took part in this rough sport when he said, speaking of the wholesale price index, "The rise of the rate of increase is downward rather than upward," push-pulling a statement that meant simply, "The index is not rising as fast as before"—though his words, if read quickly and uncritically, encouraged the hope that wholesale prices would be lower soon. There is illogic in this use of language, or at least the appearance of saying yes and no at the same time. Among less exalted speakers, the problem often takes the form of outright contradiction, as when someone *is found to have disappeared* or *turns up missing.* Certain adverbial phrases pit two words against each other in a similar tug of war: *fully devoid, highly inferior, greatly unimportant.* Related specimens include the pregnancy test that yields *positively negative results,* the golf ball that *slows down fast,* the sharpshooter who *scores a miss,* and the euphoric *down high* experienced by one who takes depressant drugs. It is doubtful that any of these expressions can be called an oxymoron in the classical sense, because to ancient rhetoricians the term meant a "witty-silly" figure used deliberately and with epigrammatic effect, as in the pregnant Greek and Latin saying, "Make haste slowly." No such cleverness is discernible in the educator who speaks of *an advance in the field of mental retardation,* the insurance-company executive who reports *a better loss experience,* the Internal Revenue official who penalizes a taxpayer for *excessive underdeclaration,* the army officer who finds himself *in the forefront of a retreat* (no doubt after his offensive *built up to a collapse*), the postal clerk who must *forward mail back to the sender,* or the meteorologist who predicts that the day's air pollution will *improve to unsatisfactory.* But the most numerous—and blindest—practitioners of push-pull flourish in commerce and economics, where *a growth recession, a house over $3000 underpriced, a negative capacity increase,* and *a slowdown in the sales pickup* are considered routine good English. Clear English, perhaps, to the inside few, but to call it good would be to touch a low point in overstatement.

Racetrack Metaphors

When Mark Twain remarked that "it is difference of opinion that makes horseraces," he may have been serious or
sardonic. He must have been thinking that like-minded people make dull company, and that there is excitement in a
sport in which those who wager and those who ride the
horses—and even the horses—disagree about the outcome of
a race before it is run. Although not everyone looks to the
racetrack for life's strongest thrills (some people find stimu-
lation in bezique or crewelwork), many of the expressions
evolved from horseracing have found their way into the
vernacular, where they try to prance but only plod in spav-
ined lameness. Thus an easy victory in any contest, say a
spelling bee, won *in a canter* or *a walk*, or *hands down* if the
spellbound jockey is so far ahead that he can afford to *relax
the reins*. The words hardest to spell appear toward the end,
in the *homestretch* or *stretch*, and the competition may go *down
to the wire*, the finalists running *neck and neck* until one *noses out*
the others and is acclaimed the winner *by a nose*, thereby
giving his boosters in the audience a rewarding *run for their
money*. Certain metaphors in this class are shared by other
sporting exertions, such as track and gambling: *in* (or *out of*)
the running, a long shot (from the difficulty of hitting a distant
target), *off and running, off to a flying start*, and the *parlay* (a
succession of bets in which the original sum and all its winnings are risked again). Certain other metaphors are also
shared, but by direct appropriation from the racetrack. Labor unions seek wage increases *across the board* (in the same
percentage for all workers), distorting the phrase used by
gamblers when they bet that a horse will *win, place, or show*,
or be one of the first three to cross the finish line. And almost
every politician, whose fortunes are as chancy as those of the
turf, borrows freely from its cant when he *bolts* his party (as
a startled horse might do) or serves it as a *dark horse* (an
unknown who is given a chance of coming in first), hoping to
turn into a *front-runner* and perhaps, if the other aspirants
agree to *draw rein* and *slow their pace* deliberately, become a

shoo-in on election day. Without this indirect help he must *jockey for position* on his own, seeking the advantage of the *inside track* during the campaign. If the tallying of votes points to a *photo finish*, he can demand a re-count, but to his supporters the result is almost as disappointing as if he had been *left at the post;* he is virtually an *also-ran,* and they have no wish to *back the wrong horse.*

Raconteurs' Clichés

Few bores can bore so thoroughly as those who tell anecdotes in language peppered—but not salted—with stuffy ritualistic words and phrases. From dais and soapbox, from rostrum and pulpit and platform, at a banquet or in his host's living room, the raconteur speaks his platitudes as if he had just created them, no matter how stale or frayed they sound to his listeners. Here we join him (reluctantly) after dinner, and hear him refer to the cocktails that preceded it as a *libation* (inevitably *preprandial*) and to the meal as a rare opportunity to *consume* or *partake of* the *viands* on the *groaning board,* at which everyone enjoyed *an elegant sufficiency.* Then he begins to tell his unctuous tales, in which the characters are not presented as *dressed* but as *attired, clad* or *garbed,* and in *habiliments* or *raiment* rather than in *clothes.* With even less respect for simple English, he speaks of a man *in the throes of* knotting his bow tie (a *throe* is an agonizing spasm, like a birth pang) or of a woman who falls overboard and *proceeds* (by choice?) to drown. The plots, which do not matter to anyone but him, may begin with a *swain* (a handsome fellow *if there ever was one*) and a *damsel* (naturally *of the fair* or *opposite sex*) who *take one look* at each other and *promptly fall in love.* This happens on *one fine day,* and next comes a *tryst* at which the lovers *plight their troth.* Before long the girl is installed as the young man's *helpmeet* or *better half* (also known as *the little woman*), and he basks in *wedded bliss,* suffused by the blessings of *a good woman's love.* The story might end here, but *fate has ordained otherwise.* The discourse rambles on until, after *lo, these many years,* the wife looks into her mirror and discovers that she has become *a woman of a certain age* and *long in the tooth.* This stimulates her *woman's intuition* to suspect her man of infidelity, and *as luck would have it* she is right. *In high dudgeon,* therefore, she packs her clothes, leaves him *unceremoniously* and *without further ado,* and *repairs* or *betakes herself* to her mother's home—where it is best to *write finis* to the *tale of woe,* if only *to make a long story short,* which the raconteur cannot bring himself to do. Since this account does not exhaust his hoard of soporific phrases, further doses are appended here as a prescription for insomnia:

beat a retreat
conspicuous by one's absence
deafening silence
dubious distinction (or *pleasure*)
from the sublime to the ridiculous
in modern parlance
in one's inimitable way (or *fashion* or *style*)
in this year of grace
little did he know (or *reck*)
little dreaming that
make a hasty exit

much to one's surprise
none other than
of which (or *whom*) more anon
on this auspicious (or *festive*) occasion
present company excepted
so rudely interrupted
to go blithely ahead (and)
to wend one's (merry) way
twist of fate
who needs no introduction
who shall be nameless
wondrous (or *curious, sad,* or *strange*) to relate

Rapid Succession

Cliché. After *in,* a journalist's description of how one event or catastrophe follows another. Replace the phrase with *quickly, swiftly,* or any other adverb that conveys the same sense without the same monotony.

Redundancies

Timidity and ignorance, mingled in who knows what proportions, account for many of the absurd tautologies that distract the reader by shunting his attention to themselves. For the writer who fears that a word he plans to use may not be clear, the remedy is to find another that will be, rather than to try to salvage his first choice with the rickety prop of a synonym or near-synonym. If the word is unclear even to him, he should look it up before attaching to it another that merely duplicates its meaning. A third cause of double-entry phrasing, worse than the first two, is the laziness encouraged by the set phrase, the pairing or grouping of words into clichés that trip off the tongue or typewriter without first passing through the mind. The effect is often ridiculous and always uncultivated. It appears in expressions like *three* A.M. *in the morning* and A.C. *current,* where the initials need no help from the elaborations that follow them; in single ideas commonly given dual form, as in *cash money, free gift,* and *Jewish synagogue;* and in the pointless use of temporal modifiers in *past history, previous experience,* and *future plans* (if these are defended as idioms, let the defenders find a defense for *predestined to succeed, to pre-prepare beforehand, to plan* or *preplan in advance,* and *to plan ahead for the future*).

Some words suffer more than others from illiterate extension: *consensus,* which embodies the idea of general agreement, turns up in various twice-over versions, such as *consensus of opinion* or *thought* and *common* or *general consensus* (occasionally a bonehead speaks of *the consensus of my opinion*); and *continue* sees its self-sufficiency destroyed in *still continue* and *keep continuing on.* The parasitic use of *together* after verbs connoting a group of a few or many—*assemble, confer, congregate, converge, gather,* and others—assaults their integrity. Among adjectives, *basic* is forced to mate adulterously with *axioms, elements, fundamentals,* and *essentials,* which are wedded to bases on their own; *brief* with *flick, outline, skirmish,* and *summary,* which are by definition short; *central* with *core, focus,* and *nucleus,* as if these might be slipping toward some periphery; and *old* with relics like *antique (n.), crone,* and *hag.* Casual speech aligns the synonyms *tiny* and *little* and puts both before *bit, sip, midget,* or *trickle,* compounding the tautology, and does the same with *great-big-huge* when it festoons *behemoth, elephant,* or *whale* with all three. The repetitiousness is rampant before and after words beginning with *re-,* as in *to reaffirm, repeat,* or *restate again* and *to retreat, return,* or *revert back.* If *new* precedes *re-examination,* we should be learning about a third or subsequent examination but not about the second; if *new* precedes *innovation,* we should ridicule the source.

Tautologies also occur in longer form. The worst ones make us wince in the presence of repetitious wording—*Federal-aid aided housing, adding additional telephones, sections glued together with glue*—and the best ones, the merely ludicrous restatements of a single thought, induce only pained smiles—*the battle unprecedented in history, the chipmunk that hibernates in the winter, the baseball game rained out because of the weather, the boycott in its second consecutive day in a row, the ghost that vanished from view, the pioneers who traversed across the prairies, the snowfall that exceeded more than twelve inches, the task that grew increasingly more difficult.*

There is no limit to such inventiveness by the timid, the ignorant, and the lazy, but the following partial list of their offenses may instruct even the offenders if they give it a *visual look* and *mentally imagine* their contributions to it, which are *really real* (see also GENERIC CRUTCHES, TWICE-TOLD CONNECTIVES, and TWOFERS):

actually authentic
actual facts
added increments
adequate enough
all throughout
another additional (visit)
baseless and without foundation
both men and women alike

both tied for first place
caucus meeting
common accord
complete and unabridged
complete panorama
completely complete
consequent result
dead carcass, corpse
emotional feelings

end result
eventual outcome
exactly identical
fictitious lie
final completion
filthy dirty (clothing)
first begin, discover, originate
flat plateau
fully intact
grateful thanks
hastily improvised
hired mercenary
hopeful optimism
implied innuendo
in common with each other
irreducible minimum
joint collaboration
look back in retrospect
meaningless gibberish
more preferable
multitude of people
mutual cooperation
natural instinct
obviously evident
original founder
outdoor al fresco (concert)
outdoor patio
personal friend

present here
present incumbent
pure unadulterated (coffee)
queer paradox
raze to the ground
regular routine (duties)
remaining remnants
shuttle back and forth
small modicum
small hamlet, village
spoken dialogue
standard cliché
stupid idiot
sudden impulse
sum total
sworn oath
target objective
temporary truce
tiny inkling
total all-out (effort)
true facts, reality
ultimate outcome
unexpected surprise
universal panacea
urban cities
usual habit
well and good
whole total (profit)
wide expanse

Restaurateur

The correct spelling, without the *n* that forms part of *restaurant*. The French parent-word connotes an eating place where patrons are *restored;* the proprietor should not be repaid with an illiterate confusion of his title with his establishment.

Rhyming Pairs

Most of these belong in slang and the common speech, and the writer's and speaker's concern with them is only to make sure that he does not unconsciously make them a part of his style. Nevertheless, they are noteworthy as the poor man's poetry, delighting his plebeian ear in the same way that ALLITERATIONS do, often crowding wisdom into a few syllables, yet not burdening him with the intricacies of formal verses such as sonnets. He enjoys the quick jingle with a compact but clear meaning. It differs from the subtler rhyming slang developed by London's Cockneys, in which the matching word is understood but not spoken—an argot that has produced wry puns like *holy friar* for liar, *trouble and strife* for wife, and *twist and twirl* for girl, alongside simple sound-alikes: *bowl of chalk* for talk, *cough and sneeze* for cheese, and *pig's ear* for beer. True rhyming pairs occur in formal writing as catch phrases meant to sum up opposing forces—*fight or flight, masses and classes, town and gown*—and in political out-pourings meant to elicit awe or fear (and votes)—*gloom and doom, needs and deeds, right and might.* Much more often, however, they are born as perky slang, live on nearly everyone's lips for a while, then find a grave in obscure dictionaries. One term of high praise in the 1920s, *the bee's knees,* is remembered by few and used by no one today, and the later *date bait,* used assiduously by the teen-agers of its day, has also gone the way of fads, to a death by surfeit. (Who remembers when a *short snort* meant a flight across the ocean, and the airborne travelers proudly called themselves *short-snorters* and exchanged autographed paper money as souvenirs? Now the *jet set* flits aloft, and in time there may arise a breed of *moon goons.*) Other rhymes that flared briefly into popularity, particularly on college campuses, include *cheerful earful, culture vulture,* and *gruesome twosome.* A few reduplications, such as *hurly-burly, fuddy-duddy,* and *superduper,* display an astonishing will to live, however informally (will the current *nitty-gritty* join them?), along with expressions that put proper names, such as *plain Jane, slim Jim,* and *screwy Louie,* into the general stock of jingle-lingo. New rhyming pairs are bound to come along and take hold briefly or for good: the pleasure all of them provide is demonstrated best, perhaps, by the poor ones that the public happily endorses—such merely assonant pairings as *chow hound, eager beaver,* and *hostess with the mostest,* and the metrically maimed *private eye.* Some healthier examples follow, not guaranteed for either elegance or long life (see also ALLITERATIONS and TWOFERS):

ants in one's pants	local yokel
brain drain	make or break
cheers and jeers (or *sneers*)	moan and groan
claim to fame	name of the game
even Steven	nitwit
fair and square	rabbit habit
fat cat	rough stuff
hell's bells	sky high
high and dry	sure cure
hot shot (or *spot*)	true blue
huff and puff	walkie-talkie
hustle and bustle	wear and tear
late, great	wheeler dealer
legal beagle (or *eagle*)	wine and dine

Rude Awakening

Cliché, describing the worst way, whatever that is, to be jarred out of sleep, sluggishness, or an unrealistic belief. A shabby-genteel term for comprehension of *the awful truth* that used to overwhelm the once and never-again maiden heroines of silent movies on *the morning after.*

Sad Commentary

Cliché, equivalent to shaking the head in disbelief or clucking the tongue in displeasure at some turn of events. One improvement would be *a sad reflection,* another *an unpleasant commentary;* but the best course is to discard both elements and begin afresh with a phrase like *an unwelcome development* or, if stronger condemnation is merited, *a reprehensible* or *hideous* one.

Scene

This bedraggled word, which properly denotes the place where actors perform or a subdivision of the dramatic work in which they appear, has suffered barbarous changes in its use, mostly in the slang senses derived from its secondary meaning of "setting" or "locale." (See also STAGE META-PHORS.) This extension sounds normal in, say, *a scene of revelry,* but it begins to be overstretched (and overused) in phrases like *the black-belt scene, the literary scene,* and *the save-the-sequoias scene.* In a further abuse of the connotation, jazzmen and hippies have adopted *to make the scene* as an obscure equivalent of physical presence where an activity occurs and often of taking part in it, whether that involves playing an instrument or puffing on a communal reefer. If such a person sets out *to make the Hollywood scene,* he may be dreaming of stardom or merely planning to see a movie. Used without a modifier, *the scene* often stands for the smart set and its antics of the moment, though smartniks have also been known to dress adjectivally *for the evening scene.* From the generalized sense of "what's happening," the word is forced to moonlight in many senseless and sceneless *scenes,* such as *the drug scene* or *the mental-health scene,* where *problem* would serve better, or, in some dim acknowledgment of Japanese cookery, *the sukiyaki scene.* The saddest treatment of *scene* appears in reports written by policemen and petty bureaucrats, who righteously abhor slang in writing but are deaf to the dull murmur of DRONE WORDS. Using the normally worded *scene of the crime* as their base, they heap on top of it the witness who was *present (at the scene),* the detective who promptly *arrived (on the scene)* and later *departed (the scene),* and so on almost obscenely until we are ready to *flee (the scene)*, as the suspect probably did, in search of a soothing *change of scene.*

Scratch the Surface

Cliché, apparently first used to describe a superficial tilling of the soil. Now it is applied figuratively to any performance that is negligent, tentative or incomplete. A book is said *to scratch the surface* of its subject (which may be oceanography), and astronauts to have done no more than *scratch the surface* of the universe. Absurdity can go no farther, nor be farther-out.

Sectional Terms

In what must be a subconscious transference, the rewards of life are often likened to a fragrant home-baked pie just taken out of the oven. This assumption would explain the use of *cut* in slang to designate a criminal's portion of loot or the percentage of a gambling pot retained by the house. The metaphor becomes explicit in the jargon of Wall Street, where we hear of *a piece, slice,* or *wedge of the corporate income pie.* In more rarefied usage, the notion of a divided circle is preserved in such clichés as *the private sector of the economy* (a genteel reference to those not on the public payroll, often made by those who are), and in the variously dismembered *segments*—of a college faculty, a civic community, a lawmaking body, and so on—that are merely *parts* or *groups* or even *factions* in fancy dress. The word *section* belongs here, too, but only in part, because its standard meanings have progressed beyond the pieplate to other forms of subdivision, such as *a sectional sofa* or *the sections of a book.* The obsolescent *slice of life,* whose inspiration should spring from a salami or a loaf of warm bread cut vertically and not along a radius, may be technically out of place in this entry, but it does support the general hypothesis concerning segmentation terms—that they envision freshness but express it in stale words.

Self

Enough has been written and argued about the propriety of *self-addressed envelope* to support an unequivocal dictum: the phrase is acceptable and accepted in the sense of an envelope addressed *by* or *to* oneself, regardless of the literal-minded who insist that only an exceptionally clever envelope can address itself. (Compare "NO" NONSENSE.) Nor is there any objection to *self* as an adjective specifying "of the same material," as in *self belt* and *self lining*; it has long been included in the jargon of seamstresses and clothes designers, however quaint it may sound to others. Compounds beginning with *self-*, however, can be constructed so easily that each one needs to be examined and justified as it arises in the mind. Those that are plainly reflexive, for example, pass the scrutiny of logic without quibble: *self-control, self-pity, self-service*, and many others link a self to the meaning of a noun in an indivisible way. The strain on thought begins when the prefix becomes a mere intensifier, as it is in *selfsame*: words like *complacent, composed*, and *opinionated* gain little besides bulk when *self-* precedes them. The problem in logic grows more difficult when *self-* is stretched to represent lifeless objects as independent agents—a *self-pronouncing dictionary* utters no sound; a *self-propelled vehicle* (robots and ballistic missiles included) sits motionless until activated by a human signal; a *self-winding wristwatch* runs down if left on a dead man's wrist—but most examples of this sort must defer to usage and usefulness, not to reason. Nevertheless, the neologism to *self-destruct* remains a barbaric mad-scientist BACK FORMATION created needlessly, because the gracious good English of *to destroy itself* would have served. A final example, from an advertisement, will show how *self-* can be forced out of control. The subject is a batch of ordinary popcorn and an appliance that not only heats the grains until they pop but, still in the role of agent, *self-butters* them. Thus far the reader can follow the intent, but then he realizes that the technique cannot succeed without a primary agent, the user, to *self-butter* his popcorn by turning on the switch.

Senior

This Latin comparative, meaning "older," carries the force of a superlative in some official rankings. The *senior diplomat present* has no superior in an assembly of fellow diplomats, either in years of service or acknowledged dignity. To refer to him as the *most senior* (the "most older"), as many newsmen do today, is to breach both protocol and good usage. (Compare MAJOR, MINOR.)

Senior Citizen

Cliché, young in years but already settled in the rocking chair of usage as understood by politicians, advertising men, and other manipulators of cosmetic words. At first the phrase was intended to flatter men and women who, despite wrinkled skins and stiffened joints, were able to vote and spend money. Now, however, as the age of retirement is reduced, many people in their early sixties and some still in their fifties find themselves in the same pampered discard pile with the true *ancients of days* and are uncertain how to *act their age*. On which birthday does one leave middle age officially behind? And are all non-senior citizens to be considered *junior citizens*? The newly hackneyed *senior citizen* stands a long way from *a ripe old age*, or the overripeness of *a dirty old man* who is *old enough to know better*, or the final regression to *second childhood*. He has a right to resent, as many do, being stuffed into this ill-bounded category and to prefer to be called, with simple dignity, *elderly* or *older* or *retired*. Two alternative designations for the group, *Teen-agers* and *seasoned citizens,* have been proposed seriously but cannot be taken seriously. Indeed, some patriarchs and grandams declare that they would rather be known as *old fogies* or *old foops,* valuing a little forthright disrespect more highly than hypocrisy.

Sense

Cliché word, not in itself but in combinations that occur too often to be welcome in good writing: *in a broad sense, in a deeper sense, in the best* or *truest sense.* A man praised as *a gentleman in a very real sense* is no more to be envied, and no easier to comprehend, than a woman called *a lady in every sense of the word.* Both sexes fare better without such trite elaborations.

Seriously Consider

Cliché, among the clearest proofs that two words are not better than one—indeed are far worse—if used together as persistently as these are. The adverb is a SPENT INTENSIFIER here, and ready to be laid to rest.

Sickening Thud

Cliché, well characterized by its first word; often preceded, appropriately, by *dull.*

Similes with As

The trouble with most *as . . . as* expressions is that they are silly similes heard too often. A few make precise comparisons, some may be called jokes, others are outright nonsense—and all endure tenaciously in the nonliterary mind, ready to serve in place of originality. Thus the idea of diligent work finds unhesitating utterance in *as busy as a beaver*, a level surface in *as flat as a pancake*, and silent movement in *as quiet as a mouse*. For humor we make do with *as big as a house*, *as cuckoo as a clock*, and *as scarce as hens' teeth*. Those that flirt with nonsense—or drown in it—include *as clean as a whistle*, *as brown as a berry*, and the heartless *as funny as a crutch*. Exuberant alliteration, and little else, seems to inspire many others—*as cool as a cucumber, as dull as dishwater, as fit as a fiddle*—although, curiously, few take advantage of rhyme (*as high as the sky, as loose as a goose*). Considering the rustic flavor of most *as* comparisons, it seems natural that animals should predominate as models; besides our dumb friends already cited, the zoo houses these: *as blind as a bat, as clean as a hound's tooth, as cute as a kitten, as dead as a dodo, as drunk as a billygoat, as dumb* (or *as strong*) *as an ox, as fat as a pig, as free as a bird, as gentle as a lamb, as happy as a lark* (or *as a clam*, whose puzzling joy must be elucidated by adding *at high tide*), *as healthy as a horse, as hungry as a bear, as mad as a hornet* (or *as a wet hen* or *March hare*), *as nervous as a cat, as poor as a church mouse, as proud as a peacock, as sick as a dog, as slippery as an eel, as sly as a fox, as stubborn as a mule, as wise as an owl*. For less specific comparisons, the vernacular relies on an all-purpose, fit-everything formula beginning with *as x*, where *x* = any adjective, and ending in *as all get-out, as anything, as the dickens, as the devil*, or *as hell* (witness: *as cold as hell*), and the milder *as x as x can be*. When *good* is the adjective, it often forms part of an idiom meaning "almost" or "practically," as in *the battle is as good as won* (or *lost*). A fresh *as* simile can still evoke pleasure or amusement: whoever dismissed a yacht race with *as exciting as watching grass grow*, or a chess match with *as absorbing as seeing a sponge die*, put wit to valid use. (See also SIMILES WITH LIKE.) No wit survives in the following:

as American as apple pie
as bald as an egg
as big as all outdoors

as black as the ace of spades (or *coal, night*, or *sin*)

as clear as a bell (or *crystal* or *mud*)
as common as dirt
as dead as a doornail
as deaf as a post
as different as night and day
as dry as a bone (or *dust*)
as easy as pie (or *breathing*)
as fresh as a daisy
as gentle (or *meek*) as a lamb
as good as gold (or *new*)
as hard as nails (or *a rock*)
as heavy as lead
as high as a kite
as honest as the day is long
as hot as blazes
as Irish as Paddy's pig
as light as a feather
as long as one's arm
as mild as mothers' milk
as neat as a pin
as nutty as a fruitcake
as old as the hills
as plain as day (or *the nose on your face*)

as pleased as Punch
as quick as a flash (or *wink*)
as red as a beet
as right as rain
as sharp as a tack
as silent as the grave
as smart as a whip
as smooth as silk
as sober as a judge
as sore as a boil
as sound as a dollar*
as steady as a rock
as stiff as a board
as straight as an arrow
as sure as shooting (or *I'm a foot high* or *you're standing there*)
as sweet as sugar (or *honey*)
as thick as thieves
as tight as a drum
as tough as shoe leather
as ugly as sin
as warm as toast
as white as a ghost (or *a sheet*)

---

*Obsolescent.

Similes with Like

All the objections to SIMILES WITH AS can be lodged against those with *like*, and one more besides. The new one springs from the confusion that besets the uses of *like*, especially when it takes on a job belonging properly to *as*, as (not *like*) it is doing today in careless or uneducated speech and writing. Although authorities have split and resplit this one syntactical hair, turning it into a tuft of split ends, a few useful and usable precepts may still be plucked from it: *like* in a comparison can always be followed by a noun or pronoun (*He cried like a baby; My son has eyes like mine*), but not by a full clause even if the verb is only implied (*They don't build houses like they used to*—change *like* to *as; The rain poured down like last week*—change *like* to *as it did*). It follows that *to tell it like it is*, often heard in disavowal of hypocrisy or lies, must be adjudged a vulgarism no matter how sincerely it is said. The use of *like* to mean *as if* or *as though* is a common and repellent practice in the United States: *I felt like he could read my mind; He sounds like he is lying; He talks like his mouth is full of marbles*. When the subject is impersonal, as in *It looks like we lost the game, it seems that* would obviate the problem and restore good usage. But the *like*-with-verb form, drawing strength from proponents of "natural" expression and grammarians who cite its occasional use by Shakespeare and later writers, is firmly emplaced in ordinary speech and will probably win full acceptance in the future. Until it does, it will remain bad style.

Carping about the misuses of *like* has terrified some writers into replacing it with absurd evasions: a reporter writes genteelly, *As with rebels everywhere, the insurgents fought fiercely*, and an executive speaks of *plant managers dressed similar to workmen*. However frightening *like* may seem, it is correct in both these examples. But one locution with *like* deserves reproach as a shameless affectation—*like so* for *this way* or *in this manner*, as in *To drive a nail, hold the hammer like so*. (For the use of *like* without a wisp of meaning, see NULL SOUNDS.) Like the *as* similes, those with *like* can be generalized informally into *like anything, like blazes, like crazy, like fun, like hell, like nobody's business,* and so on, but the specific comparisons listed below should be *dropped like a bad habit* even if their grammar does not offend:

howl like a banshee
run like a bat out of hell
read (or *know*) someone like
  a (*an open*) book

sit like a bump on a log
fight like cats and dogs
behave like a bull in a china shop

work like a charm (or *magic*)
function like clockwork
look (or *feel*) like death
  warmed over
treat someone like dirt (or *a
  dog*)
work like a dog
go through someone like a
  dose of salts
spend money like a
  drunken sailor
drink like a fish
fit like a glove
move like greased lightning
watch like a hawk
eat like a horse
sell like hotcakes
drop something like a hot
  potato
go like a house on fire (or
  afire)
wear like iron
tremble like a leaf

go out like a light
fight like a lion (or *tiger*)
sleep like a log
avoid like the plague
it is (or *was*) like pulling
  teeth
be caught like rats in a trap
run like a scared rabbit
leak like a sieve
feel (or *look*) like something
  the cat dragged in
stick out like a sore thumb
flock like starlings
kick like a steer
sink like a stone
bleed like a stuck pig
fall like a ton of bricks
roll off like water off a
  duck's back
spread like wildfire
look like the wrath of God
(do anything) like it was
  going out of style

Simple Arithmetic

Phrases borrowed from arithmetic tend to become perennial
clichés, almost as indestructible as the abstract numbers that
inspire them. The numbers, however, remain eternally
exact, whereas the popular adaptations based on them must
be considered folksy miscalculations: *what it adds up to* usually
presents a hazy conclusion, not the sum of possibilities under
discussion; *to the nth degree* suggests some vague, unspecified
extreme; *nine times out of ten* gives no assurance that a careful
count has been made; *one in a million* offers an even poorer
census of probabilities, whether the reference is to a lottery

ticket or a beloved mate; and *putting two and two together* is a numbers game for busybodies. Lately *zero* has come into fashion, as in *zero population growth* or *zero wrinkles in the bedsheets*, and one reads of various *one-to-one correspondences*, as of boys and girls at a birthday party or atomic missiles programed for each other by the United States and Russia— but these are stilted novelties uncertain of long life.

Other borrowings from arithmetic can be arranged under two headings:

1. *Plus and Minus.* In the commercial expression *$5 plus tax* the mathematical sign is proper because it symbolizes an addition. The know-noughts of advertising, however, do not sell us plain, homely cornflakes but *cornflakes plus*, as if the sign endowed the cereal with superlative qualities. The opposite sign, *minus*, is intended to outdo *without* as a word for "lacking," as in *minus her wig* or *minus his dentures. Plus* used where *and* would serve—*We have coffee, plus we talk*—does not suggest a stronger linkage, though it probably fosters a false sense of sophistication in the user; but *plus the fact that*, a boorish substitute for "besides" or "moreover," exposes him as a catch-phrase practitioner unskilled in sophisticated language.

2. *Percentages.* These belong in statistical tables and scientific assessments and should never be invoked to describe human conditions, as in *100 percent American* or the grotesquely inflated *1000 percent American*. To say that one believes in or supports another person *100 percent* is to force a valuable device of arithmetic to function incongruously in place of words—in this instance, *completely* or *without reservation*. To feel tired *seventy-five percent of the time* implies improbably long periods spent in watching the clock. The slang term *ten-percenter*, used by performers and writers in joking abuse of business agents, at least upholds reality, because their usual commission is one tenth of their clients' earnings. But no discriminating writer would report, as one reviewer did, that a certain Broadway show was played *thirty-five to forty percent*

in the nude; *almost half* would have been a more proper measure of what took place, which the review left unsaid. Did the percentage refer to a proportion of the stage business from curtain to curtain, to some of the actors but not the rest, or to how extensive or specialized an area of their bodies was unclothed? This is not simple but simpleton arithmetic. (See also APPROXIMATION TERMS and MORE AND LESS.)

Situation

A serviceable word denoting place or location, often considered in its wider setting, e.g., a city and the forests that surround it. Aside from the sense of a *job*, which it shares with *position* (both stilted extensions of their primary meanings), *situation* also signifies a combination of circumstances, usually unfavorable: a drama delves into *an embarrassing situation*, a worried businessman assesses *his financial situation*, a city council tries to alleviate *the traffic situation*. From its origin in such innocuous clichés or near clichés, the word has been transformed by overuse into a first-class DRONE, posturing in sentences but lacking the power to invigorate them. Here is a quick review of what could be called the *situation comedy* if it were not a sorry waste of dialogue:

a child who fails to learn in a classroom situation (*in class*)
a company that moves into a profit situation (*begins to make money*)
a football team in a punting situation (*forced to punt*)
ant repellent for use in an in-home situation (*in the home*)
a thief trapped in a no-exit situation (*with no way to escape*)
a danger of fire (situation) in the schools
food production in a crisis (situation) in food production
hardship due to the unemployment situation (*to unemployment*)
laboratory rats solving problems in a stress situation (*under stress*)

playing tennis in a pressure situation (*under pressure*)
an emergency (situation) requiring an ambulance
the morale (situation) in a military compound
a tie (situation) in the Supreme Court

Small World

Cliché—in full, *Isn't it a small world?*—often invoked simulta-
neously by two Americans who meet, say, in the Gobi Desert
and discover that they share an acquaintance or some trivial
link back home. As an observation in geodesy, unscientific;
as small talk, smalltime.

So, Feminine

Dictionaries devote long entries to the many valuable uses of
so, one of which may be defined as meaning "to a great
extent, expressed or understood." This is the use that appears in speech, and often even in writing, as a colloquial
equivalent of *very* or *exceedingly*. Stressing the *so* creates an
effect of girlish gushing—hence the title of this entry. Examples: *Her dress was so skimpy, My husband is so good to me, We
thank you so very much.* The same kind of trivial effusiveness is
evident in *just too cute, only too willing, such a nice* (*boy*), and *too,
too divine.* Such habits cannot be easy to cure, but the agents
of Women's Liberation and Gay Liberation are urged to try.

Spare Parts, Anatomical

Some well-worn locutions referring to the human body are
longer than they need to be: *I saw it with my own eyes; I heard
it with my own ears.* Though brazenly tautological, both sentences may be justified as conveying a folksy stress. For
clarity rather than emphasis, a person *cranes his neck* because

the verb alone can also mean the action of a mechanical crane, *knits his brows* to make sure we do not think that he is working with yarn and needles to produce a sweater, *shampoos his hair* to distinguish that ablution from the same one performed on a rug—and, in the gesture of negation, *shakes his head* for comparable reasons. (The same logic applies to the talented young lady of myth who could *wink her navel*.) A saying like *in the wink of an eye*—again folksy—would not sound right if the last three words were lopped off, though *in a wink* gets by. But no excuse, other than bad habit, exists for naming the body part after a word that defines it unaided. If a man wears a *look* of disbelief or a *smile* or a *frown*—it is pointless to add *on his face*. The reader asks, "Where else?" and feels annoyed at having had the obvious imposed on him. It is no less pleonastic to say that a man *shaves his face* (women follow more complicated rules) than to speak of a bird with *a crest on its head*. When this man dresses to go out, he may be wearing *a belt around his waist, a cap on his head, gloves on his hands,* and *sandals on his feet*. As he pauses to kiss his wife—she wears *a shawl around her shoulders*—he can *smell her perfume in his nostrils*. So with the words that follow, all of them trailing a clutter of spare parts:

blink (the eyes)
complexion (of the skin)
nape, *n.* (of the neck)
nod (the head)

shrug (the shoulders)
squint (the eyes)
wink (an eye)

Speak the Same Language

Cliché. A casually understated exaggeration, and therefore not the best language for summing up the qualities and attitudes that some people believe they have in common. If their assumption is correct, they would be less pretentious to say *think alike* or *understand each other*. If incorrect, and one or more parties refuse enrollment in the club, they would probably not be *on speaking terms* with the others.

Spent Intensifiers

Many adverbs meant to emphasize an adjective weaken it instead, because they have been used so often and so unthinkingly that their capacity to add strength is dissipated. (And note that the adjectives underlying them enjoy the same debility; compare CRITICS' CHOICES and VAGUE ADJECTIVES.) For example, a person who is *aware* gains little in awareness if his condition is described as *acutely, keenly,* or *painfully aware*; and those who rely on the false vigor of such adverbs, perhaps believing that to be *fully informed* is to be *fully aware*, are only *dimly aware* that *acutely conscious, keenly interested,* and *painfully slow* are equally worn variations of the triteness. One group of adverbs attempts to reinforce by stressing wholeness—*completely demolished, thoroughly confused, totally disorganized*—but the first phrase is tautological and all three are clichés to be shunned in the first place. Another group works through words that once denoted fear—*awfully, dreadfully, frightfully, horribly, terribly, terrifically, tremendously*—but have undergone erosion to feebler meanings; some are no more fearsome than *unpleasantly*, and at least two have defected to the opposite sense of *pleasantly: We had a terribly good time; The new typist looks awfully nice.* A third group—*actually, really, truly*—sets out to overcome an incredulity that usually does not exist except as a doubt in the writer's mind; and *really* must be singled out as a useless mannerism that should have died long ago from overwork but somehow lives on. The illiterate *real* for *very*—*It rained real hard last night*—deserves a summary interment, alive or dead, sharing a grave with *sure* misused for *surely* or *certainly* (*It sure is a nice day*) and *mighty* for *extremely* (*The sun feels mighty good*). The word *very*, as an adverb, should be used very sparingly, as should adverbs such as these:

absolutely	emphatically
astonishingly	enormously
decidedly	exceedingly
dramatically	extraordinarily
drastically	fantastically

genuinely	prodigiously
highly	purely
incredibly	remarkably
intensely	supremely
overwhelmingly	surprisingly
phenomenally	unbelievably
positively	unimaginably
powerfully	

Sports Metaphors

We are a muscular, athletic people, or like to think we are. The late Charles Atlas exploited the national contempt for the ninety-seven-pound weakling and the longing to establish virility, at least obliquely, by flexing an enormous biceps on the beach. And even though the tough frontiersmen of our past have vanished along with the frontier, we still admire the feckless barfly who offers to lick any man in the house. Whatever this fellow seeks to prove with his fists, the sports fan proves through his passion for physical contests involving others, whose actions help him sublimate some buried impulse to destroy. Collisions between players substantiate his hardihood, and their excellence at competition becomes transmuted into his own. It follows that his language will reflect these skills and exertions in metaphors that foster the same feelings outside the arena. Thus in his daily life he asks only for a *sporting chance* to be happy and a *rain check* if the opportunity must be postponed. He tries to *play the game* according to the rules, to *go the others one better*, to *come back strong* after a setback, no matter at what *stage of the game,* and not to complain when *the game is up*. At his job, where *teamwork* is a virtue, he will *start the ball rolling, keep his eye on the ball*, and occasionally execute a *grandstand play* to impress his colleagues and his boss—a stern figure who will *blow the whistle* on him and banish him to the *sidelines* if he steps *out of bounds*. Being a *good sport*, he persists in any undertaking until *it's all over but the shouting*. Several specific sports (but not all) serve as copious sources for the fan's everyday vocabulary—or, in the writer's view, limit it with stereotyped locutions, many of them permanently mired in slang. Consider these:

1. *Baseball.* An irrational person is a *screwball*, a nasty one a *foul ball*. Both kinds seldom *get to first base* (especially in courtship), and when they do are likely to be *caught off base* long before they can *touch all bases*. A successful person has *plenty on the ball* and stays *in there pitching* throughout any dispute, supporting his argument by *putting it across* directly or in the crafty form of a *fast curve* or a *slider*. With luck, he *goes the distance* to victory and wealth. He can fail, however, if his opponents attain a *high batting average* and use it to *knock him out of the box*. Looking for work elsewhere, he asks a friend to *go to bat* for him but soon finds himself *out in left field* because he cannot *field* the *lead-off* questions put to him by the employer. *Right off the bat* there are *two strikes against him*, but he recovers swiftly with a *pinch-hit* reply and knows that his application will not *strike out*. From then on *it's a brand-new ballgame*, and his paycheck fattens on an occasional *grand slam* order—though naturally, being human, he will never *bat a thousand* either with his customers or with his girlfriends.

2. *Boxing.* When labor and management meet to discuss a new contract, the true scrappers among them *come out fighting*, without so much as a pause to *square off*. Each studies his opponent's style for a weakness in *footwork* and *infighting*, and notes how adroitly he *sidesteps* a dangerous premise; each learns that, mentally, the other is neither *punch-drunk* nor a *pushover*, but can *take it on the chin* well enough to *go the limit*. This is not *shadowboxing* or a make-believe rehearsal with a *sparring partner* back in the office; the object here is not to *pull one's punches* but to *floor* one's antagonist with the *old one-two*, or with a *haymaker* or a *Sunday punch* or just a *lucky punch* (always, or usually, taking care not to *hit below the belt* and to *break clean* after a hot exchange)—in other words or letters, to score a *kayo* by sending him *down for the count* with irrefutable arguments. In a less decisive encounter one man may *lose the*

first round but bounce back and soon have the other *hanging on the ropes* and almost *out on his feet*, with no more polemics in reserve and praying to be *saved by the bell* that ends the day's proceedings. But then someone *in his corner* decides to *throw in the towel* or *sponge*, conceding the point at issue before his man finds himself *down and out*. For the loser, it may be time to *hang up his gloves* and retire from collective bargaining. The winner, however, celebrates at the home of his girl-friend (herself a *knockout*), where they turn on the radio and hear a tape-recording of the session, *blow by blow* and *round by round*.

3. *Football.* When a vote-worthy issue arises, an enterprising politician knows how to *grab the ball and run with it*; he may even *kick off* his campaign for reelection with a speech on the subject. At some point, however, he may *call a timeout* and *go into a huddle* with his associates to *tackle* the revising of his *game plan*. The right strategy will help him evade a head-on *scrimmage* with the opposition and set him on a sweeping *end run* that saves him from being *thrown for a loss*. He may be *stopped one yard short of the goal line*, but, if no one *gets his signals mixed* and the next *play* succeeds, he will *score a touchdown* at the polls.

4. *Golf.* To *tee off* a romance correctly, a young man must assume the proper *stance* and watch his *follow-through*, or his *drive* may leave him *in the rough* instead of *on the fairway*, jeopardizing the *twosome* he has in mind. The rest depends on what *stymies* or *bogeys* beset their game; but, whatever happens, they can make their way to the *nineteenth hole* and there assure each other that the outcome is *par for the course*.

5. *Track.* The *track record* of a corporation president depends on whether he can *get the jump* on his competitors despite the Federal regulations that forbid him to *beat* or *jump the gun*. So he *toes the line* and encourages his engineers to develop new products *from scratch*, hoping that his sales department will then *set the pace* in his industry. It can happen, however, that the new line of goods does not *come up to scratch* and sales *fall off the pace*, perhaps only a *hop, skip, and a jump* behind the

leader. Then the president urges every one of his employees to *get his second wind*, clear the temporary *hurdle*, and put the company *back in the race* and comfortably *out in front*.

6. *Wrestling*. A dictator keeps a *stranglehold* on freedom in his nation. He dares not relax his *grip* for fear that someone else may gain a *toehold* and use its leverage against him. If that happens, a desperate *catch-as-catch-can* struggle ensues, with *no holds barred*, until either the ruler or the rebel is *thrown for a fall*, with his shoulders *pinned to the mat* in limp defeat.

Stage Metaphors

These expressions, like the Simon Legree of old melodrama, are to be booed and hissed because they have developed, as he has, into boring stereotypes, most of them no longer *worth the price of admission* into self-respecting prose. Certain terms from the vocabulary of the theater may be considered naturalized outside it by now: *the climax* of a vacation, *an epilogue* to a disaster at sea, *an interlude* in a bridge tournament, *a prologue* to marriage. With less felicity we speak of *a dress rehearsal* for the next World War, of flamboyant lawyers who put on *an extravaganza* in court, and of a well-liked teacher who is *a drawing card* in class, probably because he *makes a production* of his lectures; and with no felicity we repeat the tired motto of the theater, *The show must go on*, in praise of almost any act of perseverance. A political convention provides the *backdrop* for many other play-acting metaphors: *the curtain rises* when the delegates assemble and *comes down* (or *falls* or is *rung down*) when they depart; at conferences held *behind the scenes* (or *backstage*), each candidate tries to *set the stage* for his nomination. It is *a bad show* for those who fail, but the successful one will *wait in the wings* until he can *come onstage, front and center*, to stand in the *limelight* (or *spotlight*) and be greeted by *tumultuous applause*. If his acceptance speech is marred by hecklers, *bad actors* who *get into the act* by *making a scene* in the auditorium, he will probably *do a double-*

take and momentarily *blow his lines.* But he *ad-libs* until quiet is restored, taking care to keep his remarks *in character,* and then resumes *like a trouper* and *follows the script* to the final *punch line,* delivering it *deadpan* or *hamming it up* for *comic relief,* as needed. His oratory *goes over big,* and leaders of the other party realize that his is *a tough act to follow.* (See also SCENE and compare MUSIC METAPHORS.)

Steady Stream

Cliché, a muddy flow polluted by overuse. Its companion, *steady procession,* is drier but no cleaner. Delete the adjective in both.

Stinging Rebuke

Cliché, alluding either to the pain caused by an attacking insect, such as a bee or a scorpion, or to the prickly reddening of cheeks induced by a harsh expression of disapproval. The noun, being stronger in sense than *reproof* or *scolding,* can hurt the ego without help from a modifier—especially this hackneyed one.

Stratification Words

The compulsion to arrange people and their fortunes by elevation, like the layers of a cake or an archaeological excavation, may win some plaudits for being tidy, but it becomes an irritant when it is imposed where its kind of neatness does not count. In ranking people according to age, for example, there is no need to resort to the sociological *group,* as in *children in the six-to-twelve-year age group,* when *children six to twelve years old* expresses the same thought with laudable simplicity. There is even less need to borrow *bracket* from the Internal Revenue Service, in which it connotes an amount of income, and misuse it as a DRONE WORD in *men and women in the divorced bracket*; or *echelon* from the armed services, where it denotes a rank in the military hierarchy or a method of deploying forces, and misapply it to any civilian organization, as in *the higher* (or *lower*) *echelons of a library staff*. Similarly the word *plane*, when it means an imaginary two-dimensional expanse or is used as a measure of spiritual attainment, should be left to specialists in geometry and morals, who are comfortable with it, and not obtruded on activities that look absurd in its company: *a higher plane of tennis* should be expressed as *greater skill* at the game, otherwise it is almost as silly as *a higher plane of shining shoes*. Professional baseball contributes a stratification of its own in such a statement as *Senator A is not in the same league with Senator B*, and show-business patois has provided the slangy distinction to be drawn between *big time* and *small time*. The word *class*, finally, encourages the vague grading of a person as *high-class, low-class, in a class by himself*. (For stratification in its least agreeable form, see LEVEL.)

Strictly

In its normal uses, *strictly* does not modify nouns. Its principal meanings, "sternly" or "without exception," apply to laws or moral codes, as in *strictly forbidden, enforced, required,* etc. Another meaning, "precisely," appears in such phrases as *strictly speaking* and *strictly truthful*. These senses, however, do not justify the colloquial extension of the word to mean "exclusively" or, in lower speech, "nothing (else) but." *We talked strictly business, Her jewelry was strictly diamonds, The proposal is strictly a gamble*—these are casual expressions to be *strictly avoided* in careful writing.

Suddenly

A habit-forming word, too often used without reason to qualify certain functions of the mind, especially the memory. It is rarely needed in *I suddenly realized*, is useless in *It suddenly occurred* to me, and is tautological in *It suddenly flashed through my mind* unless the user cares to argue that a flash can be sluggish as well as instantaneous. The pairing of *suddenly* with verbs of thought is a form of verbal automatism, imparting no stronger emphasis than the wasted adverb in *I completely forgot.*

Supreme Sacrifice

Cliché, designating especially a soldier's death in battle. Too high-flown for modern taste, though *supreme effort* (nonlethal) is endorsed and applauded by fund-raisers and athletic coaches.

Swordplay Metaphors

"Time will rust the sharpest sword," wrote Sir Walter Scott, the chronicler of bygone derring-do, and his words read like a prophecy that has come true in our time. No doubt there are places on earth where men still *live by the sword*, hacking and transfixing others with primitive cutting weapons; jeweled daggers continue to gleam at the waists of sheikhs and sultans, the stiletto and the switchblade knife retain their murderous uses, and the machete has been known to accomplish more than harvesting the sugar cane or chopping a path through the jungle. But most of humanity no longer fears the sword as an instrument of harsh coercion, and in English only a few reminders of its brutality are left, in rusted *cut-and-thrust* expressions. Blustering generals issue *saber-rattling* statements; actors play their most dramatic scenes *to the hilt*; competing pitchers in a baseball game become *locked in a duel* (a favorite cliché of sports announcers, who further exhilarate their listeners with the gruesome news that the team that scored the first run *drew first blood*); campaigning politicians *cross swords* with their opponents, frequently stepping beyond the static threat of being *at swords' points* to deliver *slashing attacks*; and government spokesmen *fence* with reporters to defend administration policies. In other borrowings from the terminology of formal fencing—also called sword*play*—we say *en garde* in mockery of the first position assumed in dueling, to warn a sham antagonist to protect himself against our sham and often frivolous assault. If the combat turns out to be a debate, there will be the *thrust and parry* of arguments, the clever *riposte* of a *rapier wit*, and the cry of *touché* by the loser in the exchange. The *trusty swords* of yore with names of their own, such as King Arthur's Excalibur and Roland's Durendal, lie rusting in romantic epics of the past; no one says *Have at thee, villain*, now, and the *affair of honor* is all but dead as a social commandment for the proud. One other kind of lethal blade deserves notice for its figurative worth in our society, and that is the *dagger*, which is unsheathed in pairs or untold numbers when men or women *look daggers* at someone they wish dead.

Take-Back Terms

A reluctance to make a full and unambiguous statement causes many writers and speakers to retract some part of it through needless qualification. It is clearly unreasonable to expel all qualifications, because honesty and preciseness often demand the limiting of an assertion: *about as sunny as yesterday* implies some change in the skies, however slight; *as sunny as yesterday* declares identical dispensations of sunshine on both days. (Compare APPROXIMATION TERMS.) The writer must decide which expression best suits his thought and the facts at hand, but if, out of timidity or false gentility, he weakens his ideas with tempering words or phrases, he is guilty of literary cowardice. The charge is valid whenever he vitiates a sentence by inserting in it an unnecessary *maybe, doubtless, perhaps, possibly,* or *probably*. The charge becomes conspicuously just when he places a rabbit-word in the same cage with a lion-word: *a fairly chaotic result; a slightly staggering revelation; a somewhat bloodthirsty antagonist.* His sin grows blacker when he uses *comparatively* and *relatively* as synonyms for *mildly* or *moderately* if no comparison or relationship to anything specific is intended or understood: *She served comparatively bitter coffee; Those were relatively pleasing developments.* And his literary soul forfeits redemption when he qualifies words that brook no qualification (see NONPAREIL WORDS): *a rather primary reason; a more-or-less immortal maxim.* Finally, as James Thurber pointed out, the queer adverb *pretty* can mock itself when it tries to soften unpretty adjectives: *a pretty hideous scar, a pretty repulsive monster.* These enfeeblements of prose form two opposing ranks. In one the subjects are diminished without being obliterated; in the other they are checked before they can attain full growth. Both make the user sound too frightened to speak forth. Here are the chief additional cravens in each class (see also PROVISIONAL OPINIONS and BASICALLY & CO.):

1. *More than nothing.*
   a bit, a little, a trifle (sometimes preceded by *just*)
   faintly
   in a sense, a way, a manner of speaking, some respects
   in some degree
   kind of, sort of (as adverbial phrases equivalent to *somewhat*, too informal for good writing)
   moderately
   passably
   somehow
   something of (e.g., a nuisance)
   to a certain (or *a fair* or *some*) degree (or *extent*)
   tolerably

2. *Less than all.*
   a good bit
   as a rule
   as often as not, more often than not
   considerably

for the most part
in general, generally
in large measure (or *part*)
in the main
largely
more than a few, more than a little (litotes or deliberate
    understatement)
mostly
on the whole
precious (*adv.*)
pretty much, well
to a great (or *considerable*) degree (or *extent*)

Territorial Words

Lovers of useless usage are having a *field day* with *field*, as well
as with *area* and other words that set illusory boundaries
around the occupations and preoccupations of mankind.
Most such territorial words enjoy good standing in the language—e.g., *disaster area* and *field of honor*—until they are
pulled down and trampled into shapelessness by the degrad-
ers. Consider *area* as a first and worst example. No sure word
or phrase can be called in to clarify its meaning in this
statement by a well-known mayor: *Now we will move much
faster in the area of Federal money* (in obtaining? in getting our
share? more than our share?). When *area* is merely a DRONE
WORD, it is wise to keep the flyswatter handy: *progress in* [*the
area of*] *welfare; a victory* [*in the*] *for civil rights* [*area*]. But when
it becomes an item in MRS. MALAPROP'S LEGACY, as in *Breast-
feeding is an area that inspires unwanted advice*, it is best to throw
away both codicil and swatter. Another space of vague di-
mensions is the *arena*, once the "sandy place" or fighting pit
in a gladiatorial amphitheater, thoughtfully carpeted with
sand to soak up blood; now the word applies most often to
the free-for-all of politics, where it belongs as a fitting metaphor. Of Euclidian space, a *circle*, meaning an inside

group—*financial circles, literary circles,* and so on—is too old in lineage to change, but the *eternal triangle,* which surely antedates the earliest axiom of geometry, has lost its hold on the tabloid mind. (For the wayward sense of *square,* see VAGUE ADJECTIVES.) The equal of *area* in uselessness is *field* when it is wasted in such expressions as *a chieftain [in the]* (of) *organized crime [field]* and *research in [the field of] ballistics.* Other territorial words fall so short of preciseness that they are almost interchangeable: whatever lies *within the domain of philosophy* may also be discovered, with hardly a change in prerogatives, within its *province* or its *realm.* The global analogue of all this triteness, *sphere*—as in *precautions in the sphere of public health* and *stability in the sphere of prices*—is a balloon inflated to the point of bursting; but *a nation's sphere of influence,* toughened by a hundred years of use by diplomats, resists the puncturing needle of cliché-killers.

These (Those) Kind

The use of a plural pronoun to modify a singular noun, as in *these* or *those kind of policemen* (or *bricks* or *lilies*), must be deplored even though some authorities smile on it indulgently as an idiom beyond the control of logic, and even though they turn to Shakespeare and other masters for sanction. Neither gifted writers nor the careless speakers of today can make broken grammar whole by fracturing it repeatedly. No matter how often *these kind* may be said habitually in casual talk, in writing it should appear as *this* or *that kind* or *these* or *those kinds.* An older rule required that *kind of* and *kinds of* be always followed by a singular noun, since a *kind* was regarded as an indivisible class; but nowadays the word is treated less strictly, so that *kinds of policemen* is permitted in good prose, and a single *kind of policemen,* while less than pleasing, is no longer an intolerable solecism. But after *these* and *those,* the use of *kind* in the singular remains substandard English, to be compared with *this here* and *that there* for rustic inelegance and with *these ones* for unpolished phrasing. (For *kind of* in the sense of "somewhat," see TAKE-BACK TERMS.)

Thing

To judge from the long entries devoted to *thing* in dictionaries, it is one of our most versatile words. It is also one of our vaguest, put to innumerable inexact uses, and its simplest one-word definition, an "entity," does little to dispel the vagueness. Nevertheless, *thing* is rooted so deeply in English idiom that one cannot condemn the whole tree because some of its branches are barren. We hear *It's a thing of the past* and perceive an ending of some sort, or *It's a good thing he told the truth* and understand that a threat or gratitude has been expressed. We say *You poor thing* or *You dirty thing* to make our sympathy or our revulsion clear. Any newest fashion is *the latest thing*, of driving importance to women who *don't have a thing to wear*, and even old Chaucer used the word, as school children still do, in the sense of "sexual organ." Turning to the plural form, we tell arriving guests *Take off your things*, and leave for vacations equipped with hunting or fishing *things*. Even in more abstract phrases we discern some morsel of substance: *all living things* (creatures); *the center of things* (where activity is liveliest); *things to come* (events of the future). Literature teems with other examples, two of which are *things that go bump in the night*, by an anonymous Scot, and *A thing of beauty is a joy for ever*, by Keats. Then where are the barren branches? Some grow in colloquial phrases too common and too tenuous to support a ponderable thought: *and things* meaning "etc.," as in *throwing confetti and things* (rocks too?—see ETCETERAS); *the thing of it is* (the obstacle? the important point?); to *have a thing* about something or someone (to feel an aversion? an attraction?). Others force *thing* to exceed its own versatility in constructions that read better with a more specific word: *All the prisoners eat the same thing* (food), *He demanded three things* (made three demands), *The outcome depends on one thing* (courage? armament? money?), *The word means several things* (has several meanings), *True love thrives on two things* (really, Mr. Chaucer). Finally there is the *thing* of current slang, deliberately diffuse and casual: *the flower thing, the love thing, to thine own thing be true*—the last an outrage, if not a sacrilege.

The writer will do well to remember that lexicographers manage to find other words to define the many meanings of *thing*. Whenever he can, he should use a more exact word in its place.

To the Nines

Cliché, sometimes preceded by *up*. The phrase is colloquial, obscure in origin but not in meaning; it connotes perfection or peacockish display, especially in clothes. Its companion, *dressed to kill*, says more than it means, but *dressed to the nines* says nothing at all except to lovers of odd language. Both should be regarded as *nine days' wonders* that forgot to fizzle out.

Toy Words

Baby talk is to be expected from young children, and welcomed and encouraged in the hope that it will ultimately develop into mature speech and writing; but some people never outgrow the liking for prattle, clinging to it as a youngster often clings to a noseless and eyeless doll. This discussion—and condemnation—does not apply to the large number of clipped or diminutive words used casually by almost everyone (*ad, phone,* and *plane* form one set of examples, *civvies, Commies,* and *movies* form another), though many fall short of elegance. Nor shall we dwell on the child's vocabulary of toilet terms (*pee-pee, wee-wee,* and all the circumventions of *defecate*), nor on his names for animals (*birdie, bow-wow, moo-cow,* and the rest of the infantile menagerie), except to reprove their use by adults. All these—not forgetting *choo-choo*—are elements of his meager linguistic apparatus and belong to him while he occupies the nursery. Later, when he is old enough to take interest in the Wild West, he will speak of the *goodies* and the *baddies*, and describe his ice-cream cone as a *biggie* or a *smallie*, at the same time that his sister writes letters containing such coyly decapitated words as *'cause, 'cept, 'fore, 'most, 'nother, 'sides* and *'thout*. Again, being minors, they are forgiven such transgressions; but as they approach majority their claim to leniency vanishes. The appellations favored by amorous couples *(dearie, lambie-pie, lovey, presh, sweetie, ums)* show them retrogressing almost to their days in *didies*. When they marry they become *hubby* and *wifey*, and presently the *daddy* and *mommy* of *buzzies* and *sisties*. No longer newlyweds, they have reached that point at which (so wicked cynics say) a *quickie* before dinner means a cocktail—a *dinky* or *dinky-poo*, perhaps followed by a *teensy-weensy divvy*. Then they sit down to *din-din* and fill their *tummies* or *tum-tums* with *yummy* food, including a salad of *crispy* lettuce. In a few hours it is time for *beddy-bye*, when everyone undresses, laying *panties* or *scanties* or *undies* aside, and puts on a *nightie* or *yommies* or *P.J.'s*. They all say *nighty-night* to one another and settle into bed, as *comfy* as can be until next morning, when the alarm clock summons them to *upsy-daisy*. If this account of unsophisticated domesticity brings tears to anyone's eyes, *all righty*, let him reach for his *hanky*. We who honor solid English will pronounce *poo-tinky* on the whole mess, get on our *horsie*, and *wave bye-bye* as we gallop toward a less mushy destination. *Yes, indeedy.*

Traditional

Nothing can be *traditional* that has not been handed down from generation to generation, and usually for centuries. The word can describe long-established moral attitudes, religious teachings, and social conventions like shaking hands, but it cannot be applied to practices not rooted in the past.

Today, however, it is being used as an unnecessary substitute for *habitual* or *customary* and thus robbed of its sense of historical perspective. The Yule log is *traditional* at Christmastime, but playing carols on the hi-fi is not, even if the carols are, and even if the hi-fi has been put to that raucous use for a number of years. Perhaps the breakdown of traditions in modern society is limiting our understanding of them, and this may explain what was (or was not) in the mind of the co-ed who wrote that a certain college auditorium *in recent years has become the traditional locus of student sit-ins.* By peering backward with myopic perception, she demoted *traditional* to a HAPHAZARD WORD, which it may soon become.

Tranquilizer Clichés

It is a popular virtue to accept disappointment *with good grace,* to *make the best* of trying circumstances, to *pick up the pieces* after a disaster and always seek to *take life as it comes.* In another version, we should *take the bad with the good,* as the Chinese, presumably, *take the sour with the sweet.* The cause of equanimity is also served by *That's the way the cooky crumbles* (from Madison Avenue) and *That's show business* (from show business)—both evidently doomed to Endurance Vile. True Stoics are rare in any age, but even those now in our midst might lose their lofty philosophical detachment if offered, at some moment of adversity, the stale solace of these *grin-and-bear-it* words:

Accidents will happen	Such is life
It happens all the time	That's the way it goes
It just goes to show (you)	There is always a first time
It's all in a day's work	You can't win them all
It's all in a lifetime	What next?
It's (just) one of those things	Win a few, lose a few
It takes all kinds	

Trigger

In its function as a verb, this is the newest addition to GUN TALK and an ever-present plaything of the press, which serves it up monotonously as a "fresh" way of saying *start, produce, result in,* and many similar expressions that point to a beginning or a cause. After a long and meek career in English as a NONVERB, during which it meant little more than the act of squeezing a trigger, the word burst into new life along with nuclear fusion (the hydrogen bomb), which requires nuclear fission (an atomic bomb) to *trigger* its ghastly discharge. The novel usage introduced the incautious *trigger-happy* era of today, in which the high cost of food *triggers a flood of protests* by housewives, a woman's perfume *triggers love* in a man, and sunlight *triggers photosynthesis* in plants. This kind of absurdity turns into sick hilarity when the missayers taint their play-word with unapprehended puns, as in *gun fatalities triggered by short tempers* or *pregnancies that trigger shotgun weddings.*

Trusting Soul

Cliché, much like its cousin once or twice removed, the *timid soul.* Try *gullible* or *guileless* for the first, with any appropriate noun denoting a person. If *coward* seems unfairly strong for the second, keep *timid* but again replace the disembodied *soul* with a whole human being.

Twice-Told Connectives

A few writers and many speakers make a habit of bullying small connectives like *and, but,* and *so,* humbling their natural strength by appending words or phrases of like meaning to them, or employing them to no purpose when the appendages alone perform the necessary linkage. The result is ineffectual bloating, as in *but be that as it may* and *so for that reason*, in which either *but* or *so* or the words that follow them should be omitted. (Compare the equally tautological *if in the event that*, when only *if* is meant, and see REDUNDANCIES.) Before reducing the swollen parts, however, it is wise to make sure that the distention is real and not apparent: *and also*, for instance, which is sometimes condemned as a pair of redundant conjunctions, is correct when *also* is perceived in its true adverbial meaning of "besides" or "in addition," as in *handsome and also strong*; and *but however*, a dropsical twinning when both words are conjunctions, is unassailable when *however* serves as an adverb expressing extent or degree, as in *but however hard he tried*, etc. Alert to such exceptions, the writer can still do his best to draw the water out of the following phrases, and restore the little words to trimness and self-respect:

and besides	but nevertheless
and furthermore	but nonetheless
and moreover	but on the contrary
but all the same	but on the other hand
but at the same time	so consequently
but even so	so hence
but in any case	so therefore

Twofers

It is at least half a century since Thomas Riley Marshall, Vice-President under Woodrow Wilson, said, "What this country needs is a really good five-cent cigar." Evidently he was above smoking *twofers*, the poor man's cigars that sold at two for a nickel. Since then this slang term has come to mean chiefly cut-rate theater tickets admitting two for the price of one—to a play or show that cannot attract an audience otherwise. In either sense twofer stands for "cheap," and that is the value to be placed on most of the pairs of words considered here. However, since some inexpensive goods are also bargains, it must be acknowledged that certain groups of verbal twofers remain above contempt—unless they are subjected to relentless overuse. The first such group relies on simple repetition to achieve emphasis, as in *again and again, out and out, through and through*; or to stress a progressive intensification, as in *harder and harder, less and less, more and more*; or to make time seem interminable, as in *ages and ages, hours and hours, years and years,* or enumeration limitless, as in *dozens and dozens, miles and miles, thousands and thousands.* Another group imitates a pendulum, its elements touching the extremes of oscillation: *back and forth, come and go, hither and thither, to and fro.* Still another deals with extents and distances: *around and around, end to end, far and wide, head to toe, high and low, length and breadth, near and far, right and left, top to bottom.* And a fourth sums up physical and moral complexities: *ins and outs, pros and cons, rights and wrongs, ups and downs.* Among miscellaneous pairs, some denote the unhurried and occasional (*by and by, here and there, now and then, off and on*)—and a few the unconditional (*first and last, here and now, now or never, then and there*). Besides all these, a few twofers are interesting because of their quaint derivations: *cut and dried*, a FOSSIL PHRASE now signifying lack of spontaneity, originally described the merchandise of a dealer in dried herbs; *hammer and tongs*, another FOSSIL, dramatizing a manner of savage fighting, goes back to the blacksmith's tools for pounding red-hot iron to a desired shape; *hard and fast*, said of rules that may not be broken, first meant a ship unable to move, perhaps helplessly aground; and *spit and image*, which is no longer taken as a tautology because people have forgotten that *spit* once meant, besides that indelicate secretion in the mouth, a strong physical or family resemblance. (One colloquial usage, of two adjectives united by *and*—*a door locked good and tight, a fabric that feels nice and soft*—must be excepted here because it is an adverbial phrase rather than a naïve pairing of related words. And a further exception must be made for natural unions that no man may put asunder, such as *ham and eggs, soap and water, tar and feathers, father and mother.*) It is to be expected that twofers and REDUNDANCIES will be found cohabiting in comradeship as units of trite speech: examples are *betwixt and between, blood and gore, fair and just* (or *equitable*), *leaps and bounds, pick and choose, stuff and nonsense,* and *whims and caprices.* The phrases that follow may be classified best as bargains in juxtaposition, easily come by when low standards prevail:

aches and pains
aid and abet
all and sundry
back and fill
beck and call (at someone's)
bill and coo
bits and pieces
blood and thunder
body and soul
bound and determined
bow and scrape
bright and early
cock and bull
cover to cover
cradle to grave
dead or alive
drunk or sober
each and every
few and far between
fits and starts
flesh and blood
flotsam and jetsam
free and easy
fun and games
give and take
give or take
hand and foot (to serve
   someone)
heart and soul
hearts and flowers
high and mighty

hill and dale
hit or miss
hope and pray
hue and cry
law and order
loud and clear
nip and tuck
nook and cranny
nuts and bolts
odds and ends
one and all
one and only
one and the same
over and done with
peace and quiet
pride and joy
pure and simple
rank and file
right and proper
rough and tumble
sick and tired
skin and bones
song and dance
spit and polish
thick and fast
touch and go
up and around
various and sundry
wait and pray
ways and means

Ulterior Motive

Cliché. A diplomat negotiating peace terms may have *ulterior* demands in mind, to be revealed at some advantageous moment, but most people see and use the adjective only with *motive*, not realizing that *secret* or *hidden* or *undisclosed* can combine with the noun to make the same accusation of wily dealing and evade the hackneyed phrase.

Umbrella

A homely, familiar contraption recently endowed with odd figurative meanings and thus with fraudulent glamour. Since an *umbrella* wards off rain and sun, it has, not surprisingly, taken on related senses, as in *a good tax umbrella* (though *refuge* or *shelter* would be more appropriate) and *an umbrella of warplanes* (though the metaphor sounds flimsy for an *air cover* screening military operations below). Now, however, we hear of *an umbrella candidate to unify the party's factions* and *an umbrella council of denominational bodies*, as if the word meant an awning or a catchall tent without the connotation of defense or sanctuary. One writer, less able than most to distinguish between style and stylish words, reported an announcement made *under the umbrella of an anniversary celebration*. No one can tell whether he meant a crafty excuse or a genial occasion, and no one need bother to ask. The problem is his, and he could have avoided it by keeping his *umbrella* in the closet, as prudent writers do, for use on rainy days.

Undivided Attention

Cliché. For most people, excepting those with complex minds and others beset by love or spring fever, or distracted by a toothache or other pain, paying *attention* is an indivisible exercise. Delete the modifier.

Unvarnished Truth

Cliché, often preceded by *plain*. The phrase protests too tritely and too much, as if truth unadorned were dirty or nasty to look at.

Upcoming

There is nothing wrong about compounding adverbs with verbal elements, provided the process is limited to what the language can accept. It is natural to speak of an *oncoming storm* or an *upswept coiffure* and, after an election, of *incoming* and *outgoing* officeholders. It is less natural, but still correct, to speak of an *ongoing debate*, although *continuing debate* sounds better in current idiom. But the word *upcoming*, long a noun meaning a literal or figurative ascent, has now been turned into an adjective by newsmen and sentenced to hard labor as a synonym for *coming* or *forthcoming*, and breezily misused with a verb in the future tense—*We will have another report upcoming*—as if the word did not refer to a time beyond the present.

Vagaries of I

Speakers of colloquial English confuse the uses of *I* and *me*, probably because as children they learned that both pronouns are forbidden in certain constructions. If it is wrong (though natural) to say *It is me*, the bewildered conclude that it must be right (and equally natural) to say *between you and I*. Each is a mistake for a different reason—the first because *is* is technically a linking verb, which cannot be followed by the accusative case form, the second because *between* is a preposition, which cannot be followed by the nominative—but both flourish in the language of those who failed to learn, or were never taught, the elementary parsing of subject and object and the inflection of personal pronouns. Since it is impractical to keep grown-up dunces after school, the following simplified precepts may help them. The first example should be *It is I*, just as Jesus spake those words in the New Testament, but this usage has been giving way steadily to *It is me* in all but the most formal writing— as have *It is she* (now *her*), *they (them), we (us),* and so on— and is almost ready for the embalmer. An exception may be noted when the basic sentence is followed by a *who* clause, as in *It is I who deserve first prize*, in which *I* sounds immodest but *me* would lead to unidiomatic discord. The feeling that *I* and *we* suggest boasting probably accounts for the illiterate self-belittling in *Me and the gang went bowling* and *Us girls sat there and giggled.* (The phrase *me too*, used by politicians as a taunt to their imitators, is illiterate when it stands for *I too* but good English as a curtailment of *That suits me too.*) The timid who shy away from plain personal pronouns have created hypocritical replacements for them: the false humility of *My wife and myself went to church* (or, by censoring the ego still more severely, *The wife and self*); the fawning of *the undersigned* addressing *your good self* in a business letter; and the vulgarity of *Yours truly was too smart to fall for that.*

Vagaries of I, Part 2

When a mother says to her ten-year-old son, "Mother knows best," and her husband adds, "Father wants you to be a good boy," both parents are guilty of a sheepish retreat into the impersonality of third-person discourse, avoiding the matter-of-fact and healthier *I*. Convention forbids the use of *I* by a newsman, who must be objective in writing his reports and suppress his personality, although he often contrives to mention himself demurely as *this reporter* or *your correspondent*, or more stiffly as *the present writer*, or by quoting a remark as made *in response to a question*, presumably asked by some unidentifiable wraith. The opposite of this cringing is displayed in the Plural of Magnificence, the *we* used for *I* by a monarch or a Pope: "We are not amused," Queen Victoria once said flatly when *she* (not *they*) *was* (not *were*) annoyed at *her* (not *their*) groom-in-waiting. The *we* of unsigned newspaper editorials implies not arrogance but a collective opinion held by the staff, and may be termed the Plural of Anonymity. A similar *we* sometimes appears in decisions handed down by judges, who speak for the institution of the law rather than as mortal beings, but they also refer to themselves ponderously as *the court.* Before we take leave of this subject, it should be added that the *we* occurring throughout this book is not didactic, as in *Today we will study the personal pronouns*; it is simply a short way of saying *many* or *most people*—neither as all-inclusive as the opening phrase of the Constitution, "We the People," nor as chummy-sickening as the nurse's *we* when she asks her patient, "Are we ready to have our back rubbed now?" (See also EPICENE PRONOUNS and compare VILLAGE IDIOMS.)

Vague Adjectives

Considering how often envy triumphs over generosity in human beings, their souls are redeemed in part by a need to express approval, and this has generated a large vocabulary of adjectives whose purpose is to praise. Their limitation is that they signify a vague enthusiasm but nothing specific. They convey emotion, not reality; hence their value as reporting is illusory. Take the trio *fine, grand,* and *great.* The first of these works well in describing a few definite characteristics like purity (*fine gold*) and delicacy (*fine print*), but what is a *fine young man* except someone hazily endowed with excellence? As for the obsolescent *grand,* it can still carry a sense of lofty dignity (*grand duke, grand finale*), but as a term of praise it belongs to our unsophisticated past, when phrases like George M. Cohan's *Grand Old Flag,* the Republicans' *Grand Old Party* and anyone's *Grand Old Man* had power to stir people without informing them. The current word, *great,* is used promiscuously by advertisers—*great hairnets, great paper towels*—and by others satisfied with inexact thought—*a great little car, a great little wife*—none of whom remember the prodigious magnitude it once connoted. (A worse fate has overtaken *square*, the bygone symbol of honesty and wholesomeness. In the old days a manly chap looked the world *square in the eye*, especially after a *square meal*, but now the word designates anyone who lacks sophistication and upholds outdated moral principles. The sense of *straight* has also been bent backward by slang: a *straight guy* used to be the same as a *square-shooter*; now he is defined negatively as one who is not homosexual and does not feel disgraced by a shave, a haircut, and a shoeshine.) A second trio—*amazing, marvelous, wonderful*—tries to register admiration through the awe engendered by supernatural phenomena, but fails by overexertion (compare SPENT INTENSIFIERS). Still another trio may be assembled by using *beautiful* and *delicious*, with *delectable, delightful,* or *luscious* in the middle to balance the sensual raptures that the other two evoke; but in calling Miss America *beautiful*, we do not help the reader to envision her and the many attributes that make up her beauty, nor in pronouncing our broiled shad *delicious* do we say anything about its texture and flavor, but merely imply that it has been prepared with skill and has not been out of the water too long. Such words, unsupported by details, have little more worth than *zowie* or *yum*, except in their superior respectability (see next entry). Although they need not be banished from the language, they should be acknowledged as mood-creating phantoms and, if used at all, accompanied by words of substance. Here are further ghost-words apprehended in the act of committing vaguery:

delicate mosaics (what colors or designs?)
exciting fashions (what excites whom to do what?)
fabulous wealth (tell it to Midas)
gorgeous plumage (fetch the crayons)
handsome décor (information, please)
ideal complexion (with imagined warts?)
impressive arguments (cogent ones preferred)
intricate carvings (floral or geometric?)

lavish hospitality (anything goes?)
luxurious mansion (with gilt-edged bonds for wallpaper?)
magnificent mountains (state size and shape)
memorable or unforgettable moment (give it time)
ornate furnishings (have some gingerbread)
palatial yacht (most palaces are too heavy to float)
spacious hall (circular, oblong, or square?)
splendid regalia (a rented dinner jacket?)
sublime scenery (send a picture postcard)
sumptuous banquet (gilded hash, and scrumptious)
superb actress (the buttered toast of Broadway)

Vague Adjectives, Junior Grade

Like their elders, young people seek ways of declaring approbation, but unlike their elders, who favor adjectives with
some sonority (see previous entry), they prefer abrupt two-
syllable slang words ending in -y or -ie. Nouns, adjectives,
and verbs do service in this juvenile ebullience—and one
conjunction, which yields *iffy*. The young did not invent the
process; it has been at work for centuries in the best English,
giving us Milton's *dewy eve*, Shakespeare's *dusty death*, and
Homer's *rosy-fingered dawn*, a literal translation of the preclas-
sical metaphor encountered often in the *Iliad*. The established formations in -y are favored by all ages and tend
toward a casual if not inelegant tone; some are even uncomplimentary—*bitchy, cheesy, jumpy*—and others, mostly di-
minutives, may be taken as reverse endearments if the context permits—*meanie, smoothie, stinky.* (The term *falsies*, for
padding of the breasts, perplexes the orderly mind; they
appear almost invariably in the plural, but are worn inside a
bra, which is invariably singular.) But most users of such
words—they include writers mature in years but not in
spirit—care only for novelty, not for etymology. From the
hoary Appalachian dialect they borrow *feisty* in its prevail-
ing sense of "belligerent" or "spirited," not knowing that its
progenitor phrase, *fisting dog*, designated a scrappy little

mongrel that broke wind. They take up *raunchy*, a modern word of no known pedigree, and change its meaning from "falling apart" or "slovenly" to "lewd" or "lecherous," perhaps through the dual sense of "dirty" but possibly because the word itself sounds obscene. They welcome the emergence of *foxy*, long used to describe a crafty act or person, as the latest synonym for sexy, and rush into print with *jeezly*, an ugly new adjective that brings the familiar *gee whiz!* closer to its paternal but still not proper *Jesus!* In the list that follows, some specimens are dying out and some have undergone resuscitation; not one commands a life expectancy worth betting on, but the species will survive as long as adolescent minds cannot distinguish applause from articulate thought:

classy	peachy
dandy	peppy
dishy	snappy
dreamy	snazzy
groovy	spiffy
jazzy	trendy
kicky	zazzy
marvy	zingy
nifty	zippy

Vast Difference

Cliché, a shabby fixture in the vocabulary of hack writers. A few differences may properly be termed *vast*—e.g., the difference between man and ape, man and mouse, man and woman—but most others vary in magnitude from picayune to colossal and should be modified by fitting adjectives.

Via

This little word, which means "by way of," fits best in sentences that describe a route or journey: *to New York via turn-*

pike; Chicago to Los Angeles via Las Vegas. The practitioners of colloquial idiom, not knowing that *via* is the Latin word for road, use it also to mean "through the medium of" or "by means of": *travel via bus; success via hard work.*

Vicious Circle

Cliché, more overworked than misused, except by those who equate it with a treadmill. Commuting to and from work is a routine, possibly *vicious* but not a full *circle* in this sense because the homeward trip cannot be said to cause the one that will be taken on the next morning. In formal logic the term is used to designate a ring-around-the-rosy argument in which premise and conclusion are employed to prove each other. A loose example might run like this: spellings in the dictionary are always correct, and their correctness is established by their presence in the dictionary. In medicine the phrase is likewise reflexive, as in (again loosely) the itch-scratch-itch sequence in which the affliction undergoes progressive aggravation. Human problems can also be locked into such a frustrating cycle, as when a man tries ever harder to ingratiate himself with others and they treat him with increasing scorn as a sycophant, but his plight is as commonplace as the cliché that describes it. Plain English would be better off without this pair of words, and thus without the tiresome puns that they inspire—*the vicious family circle, the vicious social circle*, and similar merry-go-round banalities.

Village Idioms

English in America is a far more uniform language than in England, where dialects hinder communication between any region and its neighbors except where Standard English prevails. This linguistic fragmentation occurs all over the world and is often so complete that citizens from different parts of the same nation are unintelligible to each other. In the contiguous United States, however, speech and writing have evolved into a homogeneous medium with few regional peculiarities and no inflexible strata to separate the formal style from the informal, including slang and vulgarisms. Nevertheless, we note some small indigenous departures from full uniformity—e.g., the broad *a* of *ask* in New England, the *howdy, podner* of the West, and the *you-all* of the South—and in their company we find other locutions, used in small areas or throughout the nation, that strike the educated ear as illiterate or at best substandard. Consider these three verbs in their deviant rural usage: *aggravate, expect, suspicion.* The first is made to mean "annoy" (*The boy's back-talk aggravated his teacher*), the second takes the place of "suppose" (*I expect it's nearly noon*), and the third is merely an inelegant way of saying "suspect." In these senses *aggravate* and *expect* enjoy the approval of at least one formidable British authority but find only weak favor in good American writing; and no one wastes a kind word on *suspicion* as a verb. Charity should likewise be withheld from such vernacular expressions as:

a man name of . . .	soup's on (the call to *come and get it*)
a sight (= a great deal)	
come to think	take it into (or *get it out of*)
fit to be tied	one's head
have another think coming	the cat wants in (or *out*)
I hear tell (= they say)	the (sugar) is all (= none is
I like to died	left)
in all my born days	they is (= there are)
Junior is to school	wait dinner (for a latecom-
make yourself to home	er)
she rose seven children	

A few other oddities belong here: *to wait on* (for standard *for*); *to plan on, try and, be sure and* (for *to*); and the backwoods liking for *as how* in place of *that* after *allow, being,* and *seeing*—though even the reinstatement of *that* would fail to elevate them to propriety. Further hayseed usages appear in expressions of time: *Dinner was cooking, so I set the table awhile* (in the meantime); *The ice is too thin to skate on just yet* (now or still); *What's the world coming to anymore?* (nowadays). Of outright illiteracies like *ain't, didn't ought, don't let's* (and *let's don't*), *he don't, should of* or *would of,* and forbidden double negatives like *can't never seem to* and *that wasn't no lady,* this simple mention should suffice.

Voracious Reader

Cliché, also current as *avid reader*. Both adjectives mean eager, with a deeper sense of greed or insatiability; and a third version, *omnivorous reader*, suggests the undiscriminating tastes of swine. Yet the book-fed like to refer to themselves in these uncomplimentary terms, and do not object to being called *bookworms* after the insects that devour the paste in bindings. Since these metaphors *speak volumes* to anyone who can *read between the lines*, it would be kinder to reserve *book-lovers* for gourmands of the printed page.

Warfare Euphemisms

Language joins the casualties of war when honest military words are replaced by sonorous but deceptive euphemisms. A military communiqué embellishes a humiliating retreat as *preplanned mobile maneuvering* or *falling back to previously prepared positions.* To go back no earlier than the Second World War and Pearl Harbor, our nation herded Japanese-Americans into *war relocation centers,* a bland term for *concentration camps,* which were themselves prison compounds given a denatured label. Later, to evade Constitutional and diplomatic technicalities, our forces engaged in a *police action,* not a war, while fighting in the so-called *Korean conflict,* and afterward shed still more blood during the vapidly named *Vietnam era.* Various specific evils in the Southeast Asian struggle were made to masquerade in pretty words—e.g., *protective reaction* for an air raid intended to annihilate, *resources control* for defoliation, and the happy-hearted *new life hamlet* for a refugee camp.

Wastes of Time

We are all imprisoned in one fleeting, ever-changing "now" that hurries us along in a single direction, so we join with the poets and gnomic finger-waggers in accepting our bondage and palliating it with toothless old saws like Horace's *carpe diem* and Benjamin Franklin's *time is money*. A well-known sundial inscription—*It is later than you think*—gives us similar advice, unasked for and too depressing to be counteracted by any smirking optimism—e.g., *I count none but sunny hours*— that we find on other sundials. Another primitive timepiece, the hourglass, is the property of Father Time, who counts the *sands of life*. Less gloomily, we *pass the time of day* by chatting with others, bestir ourselves to action (and *high time*) when *time is running out* on our plans, *beat, buy, kill, make,* or *mark time* according to the occasion, work *around the clock* when we must and *against time* in emergencies, acknowledge that *only time will tell* what we accomplish, and recollect ecstatic thrills when *time stood still,* usually in the *small hours* (*wee hours* is for wee thinkers) of the night. Not that life guarantees us *never a dull moment,* but it indeed *has its moments* and occasionally, *on a moment's notice,* may present us with our *big moment,* which, if it comes at a propitious *psychological moment,* can lead us, like matadors, to a triumphant *moment of truth.* Life also has its *hours*—the *darkest* and *finest,* as well as the Biblical *eleventh hour,* the *witching hour* inspired by Shakespeare's "witching time of night," and any warlord's *hour of decision,* the *zero hour* for an assault that may win him glory in his native land as *the man of the hour,* if not *of the moment* or *the year.* But there is no evading of the *ravages of time;* it seems that only Time withstands the *test of time.* Nor can we ever reverse the *march of time,* because there is no way that mortals can *turn back the clock*—except for those illusory sixty minutes when Daylight Saving Time comes to an end.

Besides all these time-worn expressions, the writer must also guard against the many good, plain phrases sullied by tautological elaboration, most commonly by the heaping on of four words—*course, period, space,* and *time*—that waste everyone's time. Here are some examples, with the dross marked for disposal (see also INFINITY PHRASES, MATTER, and NOW):

during the (course of the) journey
in (the course of) a few years
in (a period of) half an hour
in a short (space of) time
a (time) delay in the proceedings
on a different (time) schedule
the (length of) gestation (time)
in a month('s time period)
a news conference during which (time)

Water Metaphors

Water, a substance indispensable to every form of life, fills a reservoir of trite expressions in English, many of them colloquial or slang, which need not be considered indispensable. The Biblical *water of life* may be essential to eternal salvation, but the phrase in its later meanings—brandy, gin, whiskey—promises only a temporary regeneration which, if sought too recklessly, can lead to a life *on the (water) wagon.* In less cosmic usages, a tyro is urged to *get his feet wet* in the figurative water enjoyed by those already *in the swim* of popular activities, or to *take the plunge* into graver uncertainties like those in *the sea of matrimony.* It is unwise for a nonswimmer to *go off the deep end* and find himself *out of his depth* and *in over his head,* struggling to *stay afloat* or at least to *keep his head above water* and avoid being *swamped;* but a self-reliant chap will *swim upstream,* defying established opinion, or, at the edge of the sea, will *breast the waves* of ill will emanating from conformists. Much depends on the *ebb and flow* of events: if he succeeds in asserting his independence, he will ride triumphantly *on the crest of a wave;* if he fails, his reputation will reach a *low ebb* and he will be *in hot water* with society—unless he can *stem the tide* of its disapproval by doggedly *wading through* his views until he proves that they are not *all wet* but sound enough to *hold water.* (See also NAUTI-CISMS.)

Weather Metaphors

The weather is a notoriously fickle blessing, capable of changing many times between one sunrise and the next, but our clichés based on weather remain steadfast, like *the calm in the eye of the hurricane.* A few abstract meteorological metaphors—e.g., *an atmosphere charged with suspicion* and *a climate conducive to meditation*—deserve respect because the words work smoothly in their acquired senses. The word *weather,* although faultless as a general term, provides some variously strained extensions: the *fair-weather friends* whom no one needs, the *heavy weather* visited on a play by an unkind critic, the debilitation of being *under the weather,* and the need to *keep a weather eye open* for trouble and to *weather the storm* or *shock* when the trouble strikes. The strain grows worse when specific weather-reading instruments are given make-believe jobs, as when the popularity of pornographic writings becomes the *barometer* of human prurience, or when the voters in Maine are transformed into a collective *weathervane* signaling *which way the political wind blows.* (The simplest way to foretell the result of an election is to toss up *a straw in the wind,* provided no unforeseen trend is *in the wind,* no *ill wind* or *winds of change* are blowing, and the electorate has not elected to *throw caution to the winds* and vote for the *windiest* candidate.) The literal manifestations of weather generate other figurative clichés almost in a *torrential downpour.* We save our money against *a rainy day, shower affection* or *praise* when circumstances move us, and sometimes feel *snowed under* by our work. If daydreaming on the job leaves us *in the clouds,* we may fail to notice the menacing *clouds on the horizon* and may misread the *clouded outlook,* to find ourselves *under a cloud* when the reverie ends and the boss is sputtering beside us. Alertness is also advisable during a *gathering storm* at home, especially in the deceptive *calm before the storm,* when it is easy to overlook *storm warnings;* depending on the misdeeds we must explain, we should brace for a *storm of controversy* or *protest,* after which the angry one may *storm out* of the house. While waiting for the tantrum to *blow over* and a reconciliation to *clear the air,* we will do well to contemplate some other *weather-beaten* terms:

blue-sky law	out in the cold
bolt from the blue	out of a clear blue sky (or
breezy manner	*out of the blue*)
gales of laughter	rain or shine
hail of bullets	sunny disposition
long hot summer	whirlwind courtship
not the foggiest notion	

Welcome Relief

Cliché, to be scrapped *with a sigh of relief.* Omit the adjective, or substitute any other denoting pleasure; e.g., agreeable, delightful, pleasant.

When All Is Said and Done

Cliché, sometimes beginning with *after* instead of *when,* but with no change in meaning. Both versions, like the shorter *after all,* introduce a self-serving conclusion with a testy undertone of "I don't care what anyone says." Good words to avoid in civilized discourse. (Compare ALL ABOUT ALL.)

Wide Variety

Cliché. Width makes a poor measure of variety; if it is indeed greater than usual, call it *rich* or *abundant,* but do not lurch from one cliché to another by changing *wide* to *endless.*

Wildlife Metaphors

In this Age of Conservation, when it is meritorious to be
kind to all wild creatures, we continue to abuse them in
tiresome legends and metaphors, applying their habits and
qualities to human behavior and even perpetuating outright
lies about them: no crocodile ever wept, no elephant ever
displayed total recall, and no ostrich ever buried its head in
the sand, though the *laughing hyena* comes by his name more
honestly, through his offensive cacchinations at cocktail parties. Pursuing our human preoccupation with *nature in the
raw,* we encounter many other forms of wildlife domesticated
in our figures of speech, both those of respectable English
and those of slang, and forced to serve mankind as tame
clichés; and too often the change in habitat has made them
scruffy literary pets. Thus lawyers *badger* witnesses in court,
reporters (often mere *cubs*) *ferret out* suppressed news, grand-
masters *lock horns* at chess, and thieves *play possum* when a
policeman walks by. (The Philadelphia Zoo once had to
deal with a *wildcat strike.*) A card player who *bucks the tiger* at
faro, playing against the bank, soon realizes that he has a
dangerous *tiger by the tail,* not Chairman Mao's *paper tiger.* If
he wins he leaves with the *lion's share* of the stakes; if he loses
he withdraws to *lick his wounds.* The jungle enlarges our stock
of slang with *monkey business, monkeyshines,* and the cruel *monkey on the back* that burdens drug addicts. The *monkey suit* is
worn by workingmen attending formal dinners, where they
ape the manners of aristocrats even though at home they *wolf*
their food. At some point they meet the *social lion* of the
occasion, who has a *social butterfly* on each arm. His haughty
condescension has them *buffaloed* at first, but then they *bristle
with indignation* and turn away with their *hackles raised.* At last
they find a humbler friend, greet him with a *bear hug,* and
settle down to the dissipations of *stags* turned *night owls.* The
modern bestiary also lists the *bears and bulls* of Wall Street
and the *hawks and doves* of wartime policy. (See also BARN-

YARD METAPHORS and FISHERY TERMS.) Many more birds, beasts and other untamed things live caged in our language, no longer heeding *the call of the wild*. Here are a few:

a bee in one's bonnet	frog in one's throat
bird's-eye view	hornets' nest
a bug in one's ear	snail's pace
as the crow flies	squirrel away
eagle-eye(d)	weasel words
feather (or *foul*) one's nest	wild-goose chase

-wise, Unwise

Spurious adverbs ending in *-wise* continue to pollute our vocabulary. The suffix does find honorable employment in two usages. One, related to *-ways*, forms an adverb meaning chiefly "in the manner of" (*crabwise, fanwise*); the other forms an adjective, often hyphenated, signifying "wise in the subject of" (*a bridle-wise horse, a ring-wise pugilist*). Benjamin Franklin juxtaposed the two formations, correctly and with a point, in *Poor Richard's Almanac:* "Some are weather-wise, some are otherwise." The indefensible use of *-wise* betrays contentment with loose coinage and looser thought, as if the suffix could be contorted to denote "as regards" and attached to any handy but hapless noun. Consider the crudity of *excellent bread vitaminwise* and *long-wearing shoes heelwise*.

Woefully Inadequate

Cliché, appealing to the *woefully ignorant* but better expressed as *sadly* or *deplorably inadequate*. The adverb is related to *dreadfully, tremendously* and similar woebegone words (compare SPENT INTENSIFIERS).

Wordy Verbs

Many robust verbs turn flabby when stretched out by circumlocution. The rules of grammar are elastic enough to survive the strain, but the resulting locutions are best left to those who use them—who like to fill their mouths and minds with needless words. For example, nothing is gained—indeed conciseness is lost—by saying *to come to the realization* and *to reach an agreement* when *to realize* and *to agree* will serve more economically. The longer versions may be justified occasionally, when the nuance of gradual attainment must be brought out, but it is always advisable to consider the shorter verb form first. Thus anyone who *has the capability of jogging five miles* should conserve his breath by cutting back to *can jog,* and if he *places emphasis on pushups* he will improve the tone of his English, and probably of his muscles, by saying *emphasize.* The verb *to make* encourages this flaccid phrasing with noun forms of several other verbs: *to make mention of* (to mention); *to make a decision, a determination, a judgment* (to decide, determine, judge). But worst of all is the verb *to be* in combination with adjectives, prepositional phrases, and occasionally nouns: *to be dependent on* (depend on); *to be in possession of* (to have); *to be the recipient of* (to receive). This stretching can be carried to outlandish lengths, as when an engine is said *to be highly consumptive of fuel* (uses too much) or a law is assailed as *not dispositive of the problem* (fails to control or solve it, but better ask the assailer what he means). Here are some other inflated expressions used after *to be,* clearer in meaning than the last two examples, but still the products of wordy language:

applicable to (apply to)
at variance with (*conflict with* or *belie*)
cognizant of (*notice* or *acknowledge*)
commendatory of (*praise* or *commend*)
cooperative with (cooperate with)
curative (*adj.*) of (cure)
deserving of (deserve)

desirous of (want or desire)
enamored of (love)
fearful of or that (fear)
hopeful of or that (hope)
in agreement with (agree with)
in a position to (can)
in conflict with (oppose or contradict)
indicative of (indicate)
injurious to (harm or damage)
in readiness for or to (be ready)
in violation of (violate, e.g., fire regulations)
of importance to (be important)
perceptive of (perceive, e.g., a falsehood)
productive of (produce, e.g., good crops)
reflective of (reflect, e.g., international relations)
reliant on (rely)
representative (*adj.*) of (represent)
resident (*adj.*) in or at (*reside* or *live in or at*)
suggestive of (suggest)
under the necessity of or to (*must* or *have to*)

You Know

Perhaps the worst plague that ever infected English is raging unchecked today. The cause is the two-syllable microörganism *you know,* which has penetrated and pockmarked the conversation of men and women who should be immune to its devastations. The effect, among the afflicted, is that every explanation or opinion, and almost every statement of fact, is preceded, interrupted, and often followed by a gratuitous *you know,* through which the speaker seeks some nameless reassurance against the terrors of plain talk: *It's, you know, time for my, you know, piano lesson; This county always votes, you know, Republican.* The ailment must be diagnosed as insecurity; the speaker fears that his words may be unclear, even if he only remarks that *It looks like, you know, rain.* He almost apologizes for not knowing and hopes that the listener will, somehow, grasp the thought. In older days *you know* did convey an unexpressed meaning between intimates, like a wink or a nudge in the ribs; now it conveys a compulsive unsureness, epidemic in range and infuriating to anyone with an ear for healthy English.

INDEX

:

finesse, 111
finger-licking good, 43
finis, 123
finishing touches, 41
fire, hang, 55
fire, running, 85
fire, under, 55
fireplug (toilet), 23
firing line, 55
first and foremost, 11
first and last, 160
first begin, discover, originate, 126
first, last and always, 67
FISHERY TERMS, 42
fish eye, 42
fish for compliments, to, 42
fish in the sea, plenty of, 42
fish in troubled waters, to,
  42
fish, kettle of, 42
fish or cut bait, 42
fish out of water, a, 42
fish, poor, 42
fish story, 42
fish to fry, other, 42
fish-wrapper, 42
fishing expedition, 42
fishy, 42
fisting dog, 167
fit-printable, 6
fits and starts, 161
fit to be tied, 170
flab, 18
flabbergast, 28
flagrant violation, 69
flash in the pan, 55
flat plateau, 126
flay, to, 76
flesh and blood, 161
flip of a coin, 51
floatel, 113
FLOATING ADVERBS, 42
floor, to, 144
flotsam and jetsam, 161

flustrate, 28
fly off the handle, 116
fly out the window, 33
flyby, 65
flying colors, with, 93
flying start, 121
focus, 105
focus attention, energy, 105
focus of debate, 105
focus of heroin traffic, 105
focus of an inquiry, 105
focus on personalities, 105
foggiest notion, not the, 175
foibles and follies, 11
follow the script, 147
follow the scent, 62
follow-through, 145
fond farewell, 11
food for thought, 44
FOOD METAPHORS, 43
footloose and fancy-free, 11
footwork, 144
for a fact, 46
for all concerned, 9
for all one knows, 9
for all to see, 9
"FOR" BETTER, "FOR"
  WORSE, 46
for certain, 46
for cheap, 46
for free, 46
for fun, 46
for gratis, 46
for honest, 46
for jollies, 46
for keeps, 46
for kicks, 46
for laughs, 46
for nothing, 46
for real, 46
for serious, 46
for sure, 46
for the best, 46
for the birds, 46
for the book, one, 46

for the life of one, 64
'fore, 156
fore and aft, 93
forefront of a retreat, in the,
  120
foreseeable future, 57
forlorn hope, 47
formulate, 59
fortuitous, 59
fortunately, 43
fortune smiles, 51
forward mail back to
  sender, 120
FOSSIL PHRASES, 46
foul one's nest, 177
found to have disappeared,
  120
four-flusher, 112
four winds, to the, 64
foxy, 168
fraction of, a, 104
frailment, 114
frame of reference, 73
frankly, 61
free and easy, 161
freedom-loving dictator-
  ships, 56
free gift, 124
freeze in the price of fresh
  meat, a, 90
friend or foe, 11
frightfully, 142
fringe benefits, 49
frivol, to, 18
frog in one's throat, 177
from a freight point of view,
  72
from A to Z, 50
from ear to ear, 50
from soup to nuts, 50
from the military viewpoint,
  72
from the standpoint of, 72
from the sublime to the ridiculous, 123

goodies, 156
goose, to, 19
gorgeous, 166
gourmet, 5
grand, 165
grand and glorious, 12
grand duke, 165
grand finale, 165
Grand Old Flag, 165
Grand Old Man, 165
Grand Old Party, 165
grand slam, 111, 144
grandee, 37
grandstand play, 143
grantedly, 43
GRAS, 4
grateful thanks, 126
grave concern, 54
gravitate, 118
gravy train, 45
great, 165
great-big-huge, 125
great little car, wife, 166
greatly unimportant, 120
greed, 18
greet, to, 79
gregare, to, 18
gift of gab, the, 7
grimace, to, 80
grim determination, 54
grin and bear it, 157
grip (n.), 146
gripping, 29
groan, to, 79
groaning board, 122
groovy, 168
groundless objections to
    strip mining, 90
group, 147
group, age, 147
grow (something) up great,
    to, 7
growl, to, 79
growth recession, 120
gruesome twosome, 127

grumble, to, 79
grunt, to, 80
grunt and groan, 12
guarded optimism, 25
guesstimate, 113
guest, to, 96
guest-host, to, 96
guest-star, to, 96
guffaw, 80
guidance counselor, 99
gumption, 28
gun, big, 84
gun for, 55
gun, hired, 55
GUN TALK, 54
guns, go great, 55
guns, spike the, 55
guns, stick to one's, 55

H, initial, 55
habiliments, 122
hackles raised, 176
hail, to, 76
hail of bullets, 175
hale and hearty, 12
half-baked, 44
ham and eggs, 160
ham it up, to, 147
hammer and tongs, 160
hand and foot, 161
hand, chuck, throw, toss in
    one's, 111
hand is quicker than the
    eye, the, 104
hand, pat, 112
hand, tip one's, 111
handsome, 166
hang on the ropes, 145
hang up one's gloves, 145
hangs by a thread, one's
    life, 30
hangdog, 20
hanky, 156
HAPHAZARD PHRASING, 56
HAPHAZARD WORDING, 57

happens all the time, it, 157
happenstance, 113
happily, 43
hard and fast, 160
hard-boiled, 45
hard way, the, 51
hardening of political arter-
    ies, 81
harder and harder, 160
hardly enough, 15
harp on, to, 91
hassle, 28
hastily improvised, 126
hasty exit, 123
hate, to, 63
have a convulsion, fit, heart
    attack, 81
have another think coming,
    170
have at thee, villain, 150
have no doubt, 118
have no parts of, 61
have the capability, to, 178
have the courage of one's
    convictions, 60
have the impression, 118
hawk (n.), 176
hayburner, 28
haymaker, 144
haywire, 28
head (toilet), 23
head, lose one's, 64
head off, shout, snore, yell
    one's, 64
head to toe, 160
heads or tails, 51
health and happiness, 12
hear oneself think, 117
hear tell, 170
hear with one's own ears,
    140
hearing handicapped
    teacher, 99
heart and soul, 161
hearts and flowers, 161

in conflict with, to be, 179
in connection with, 1
in depth, 29
in excess of, 89
in fact, 62
in general, 152,
in insufficiency of, 89
in lieu of, 69
in no uncertain terms, 66
in one's estimation, judgment, opinion, view, 118
in orbit, 119
in perpetuity, 67
in point of fact, 62
in possession of, to be, 178
in practice, 21
in principle, 21
in readiness, to be, 179
in reference to, 1
in regard to, 1
in relation to, 1
in respect of, 1
in so many words, 66
in store for, to be, 57
in the area, neighborhood, region, vicinity of, 14
in the process of, 34
in the range between, 34
in the rough, 145
in the throes of, 122
in the X range, 14
in the wake of, 93
in there pitching, 144
in tow, 93
in truth, 62
in violation of, to be, 179
-IN COMPOUNDS, 65
-in, beach, 66
-in, bed, 66
-in, cook, 66
-in, crab, 66
-in, dance, 66
-in, gay, 66
-in, kneel, 66

-in, laugh, 66
-in, love, 66
-in, pray, 66
-in, puff, 66
-in, read, 66
-in, scream, 66
-in, sing, 66
-in, sit, 66
-in, slim, 66
-in, smile, 66
-in, smoke, 66
-in, swim, 66
-in, think, 66
incandescent, 29
inch up, to, 75
incoming, 163
increasingly more difficult, 125
incredibly, 143
indefinite period, an, 104
indelve, 31
indescribable carnage, 35
indestructible, 94
indicate, to, 78
indications, 61
indicative of, to be, 179
individual, 32
ineffable contempt, 36
inexpressible sorrow, 35
infanticipate, 113
infighting, 144
infinite, 95
INFINITY WORDS AND PHRASES, 67
informed estimate, 36
inimitable fashion, style, way, 123
injurious to, to be, 179
ink a pact, to, 75
inklings, 61
inquire, to, 78
ins and outs, 160
insecticide, 118
inside track, 122
insinnuendo, 114

intensely, 143
intensive, 59
intentions, 60
interlude, 146
interpretate, to, 19
interrupt, to, 79
intricate, 166
intrinsically, 21
irreducible minimum, 126
irregardless, 113
ish kabibble, 26
it goes without saying, 35
it is I, 164
it is me, 163
it seems to me, 118
it strikes me that, 118
-IZE, 67

jackpot, 50
jawbone, to, 97
jazzy, 168
jeezly, 168
jell, to, 45
Jesus!, 168
jet, to, 96
jet set, 127
Jewish synagogue, 124
jim dandy, 28
jockey for position, to, 122
Joe Blow, 77
jogathon, 78
john, the, 23
John Doe, 77
joint collaboration, 126
joker, 111
judge and jury, to be, 12
judge by appearances, 60
jump the gun, 145
jumpy, 167
junior citizen, 132
just now, 100
just yet, 171

kayo, 144
keen-agers, 132

pending the outcome, 69
penetrating analysis, 29
penny-ante, 112
people, places and things,
  109
peppery, 43
peppy, 168
percent, 138
percent in the nude, 138
percent of the time, 138
percent, one hundred, 138
percent, one thousand, 138
percentage of, a, 104
percenter, ten-, 138
perceptive of, to be, 179
perfect health, in, 81
perform, to, 104
perhaps, 150
permanize, to, 68
personal friend, 126
perspire, 22
pesky, 28
PET, 4
pet aversion, hate, peeve,
  109
petrified, 64
phenomenally, 143
Philadelphia Eagles de-
  clared underdogs, 90
phone (n.), 155
phone, to, 96
PHONY CONTEXT, 109
photo finish, 122
pick and choose, 161
pick up the pieces, 157
picture, 106
picture, budget, 106
picture, in the, 106
picture, mixed, 106
picture of health, 106
picture of, the, 106
picture, out of the, 106
picture, pretty as a, 106
picture, profit, 106
picture, weather, 106

pie in the sky, 44
pie, piece (slice, wedge) of
  the corporate income,
  130
piece of one's mind, a, 66
pierced earrings, 87
pinch-hit, 144
pinned to the mat, 146
pins and needles, on, 103
pipe, to, 80
piping hot, 44
pizza pie, 83
P.J.'s, 156
place emphasis on, to, 178
plain Jane, 127
plan ahead for the future,
  124
plan, preplan in advance,
  124
plan on, to, 170
plane, 148, 155
plane, higher, 148
plans, 61
play, 145
play around, 110
play both ends against the
  middle, 110
play by ear, 91
play fast and loose, 110
play into the hands of, 110
play possum, 176
play second fiddle, 91
play the angles, 24
play with dynamite, 110
play with fire, 110
PLAYING-CARD METAPHORS,
  110
plight one's troth, 122
plum loco, tuckered out, 28
plunge, to, 75
-plus, 89
plus, 138
plus, cornflakes, 138
plus tax, 138
plus the fact that, 138

plus we talk, 138
point about acupuncture,
  the, 90
point-blank, 55
point of view, 71
poker face, 112
polarize, to, 118
police action, 171
politicize, 68
polyreferential semantics,
  29
poo-tinky, 156
pop into the oven, 44
popollution, 114
PORTMANTEAU WORDS, 112
port wine, 83
positive genius, a, 87
positively, 143
positively negative, 120
possible broken nose, 86
possible life sentence, 86
possibly, 150
postmaster, 98
post no bills, 94
POSTURE, 114
posture, earnings, 115
posture, glut, 115
posture, hostile, 114
posture of inter-American
  relations, 114
posture on abortion, 114
posture, tight-credit, 115
posture, to lose, 115
pot luck, take, 44
pot shot, 62
powder dry, keep one's, 85
powder one's nose, 23
powerfully, 143
practical flood of mail, a, 87
practically nil, 15
praise to the skies, 64
prayerfully, 43
precious, 152
predestined to succeed, 124
PREGNANCY EUPHEMISMS, 115

strictly avoided, 148
strictly business, 148
strictly diamonds, 148
strictly enforced, 148
strictly forbidden, 148
strictly required, 148
strictly speaking, 148
strictly truthful, 148
strike out, to, 144
stringbean, 45
strong medicine, 81
strong silent man, 35
structure (n.), 35
stuff and nonsense, 161
stupid idiot, 126
style (n.), 35
stymie, 145
sub-host, to, 97
sublime, 167
subsequent to, 69
substantially, 21
such a nice, 140
such is life, 157
sudden impulse, 126
suddenly, 148
suddenly flashed, occurred,
    realized, 149
suggestive of, to be, 179
suicide, to, 98
suit, to follow, 111
suit, long or short, 111
sum and substance, 12
sum total, 126
sumptuous, 167
sunk, to be, 93
sunny disposition, 175
superb, 167
superduper, 127
superette, 113
superific, 114
supposedly, 43
supreme, 95
supreme effort, 149
supreme sacrifice, 149

supremely, 143
sure cure, 128
sure is, it, 142
surface, to, 93
surprisingly, 143
suspected heroin, 87
suspicion, to, 170
suspicions, 60
swain, 122
swallow the dictionary, 117
swamped, to be, 173
swear a blue streak, 117
sweat, to, 22
sweep under the rug, 117
sweet, 43
sweetie, 156
swellegant, 114
swim, in the, 173
swim upstream, 173
swingles, 114
sword, live by the, 149
sword, trusty, 150
swords, to cross, 150
swords' points, at, 150
SWORDPLAY METAPHORS,
    149
sworn oath, 126
sympathize, to, 79
symphony of scorn, 91
system, 35

table, to, 96
tack, take a new, different,
    wrong, 93
tackle, to, 145
tail between one's legs, with
    one's, 20
TAKE-BACK TERMS, 150
take it into one's head, 170
take it, to, 118
take it on the chin, 144
take life as it comes, 157
take my word, 62
take one look, 122

take one's medicine, 82
take the bad with the good,
    157
take the bait, 42
take the plunge, 173
take under advisement, 70
takes all kinds, it, 157
tale of woe, 123
talk through one's hat, 117
talk turkey, 19
taps, 85
tar and feathers, 160
target, line up a, 55
target objective, 126
target, right on, 55
tarot cards, 53
tart, 45
tartly astringent, 29
task force, 85
taste (n.), 104
taunt, to, 79
taut, 29
tea, not one's cup or dish of,
    45
teamwork, 143
tear one's hair, 64
tee off, 145
teensy-weensy, 156
telescoop, 114
telethon, 78
television, 113
tell the truth, to, 62
temporary truce, 126
tense, 29
tentative teeth, 87
tenterhooks, on, 103
terribly, 142
terrifically, 142
TERRITORIAL WORDS, 152
terse, 29
Textron, 77
thankfully, 43
thanks a million, 63
that sort of thing, 39